Rossiter Johnson

Phaeton Rogers

A Novel of Boy Life

Rossiter Johnson

Phaeton Rogers
A Novel of Boy Life

ISBN/EAN: 9783337029500

Printed in Europe, USA, Canada, Australia, Japan

Cover: Foto ©Thomas Meinert / pixelio.de

More available books at **www.hansebooks.com**

A NOVEL OF BOY LIFE

BY

ROSSITER JOHNSON

ILLUSTRATED

NEW YORK

CHARLES SCRIBNER'S SONS

743 AND 745 BROADWAY

1881,

CONTENTS.

CONTENTS.

LIST OF ILLUSTRATIONS.

PHAETON ROGERS.

CHAPTER I.

A MORNING CANTER.

NOTHING is more entertaining than a morning canter in midsummer, while the dew is sparkling on the grass, and the robins are singing their joyful songs, and the east is reddening with the sunrise, and the world is waking up to enjoy these beautiful things a little, before the labors of the day begin.

And here is one of the many advantages of being a boy. When ladies and gentlemen ride horseback, it is considered necessary to have as many horses as riders ; but an indefinite number of boys may enjoy a ride on one horse, all at the same time ; and often the twenty riders who walk get a great deal more fun out of it than the one rider who rides. I think the best number of riders is three—one to be on the horse, and one to walk along on each side and keep off the crowd. For there is something so noble in the sight of a boy on a horse—especially when he is on for the first time—that, before he has galloped many miles, he is pretty certain to become the centre of an admiring throng, all eyes being turned upon the boy, and all legs keeping pace with the horse.

It falls to the lot of few boys to take such a ride more than once in a lifetime. Some, poor fellows! never experience it at all. But whatever could happen to any boy, in the way of adventure, was pretty sure to happen to Phaeton Rogers, who was one of those lucky fellows that are always in the middle of everything, and generally play the principal part. And yet it was not so much luck or accident as his own genius; for he had hardly come into the world when he began to try experiments with it, to see if he could n't set some of the wheels of the universe turning in new directions. The name his parents gave him was Fayette; but the boys turned it into Phaeton, for a reason which will be explained in the course of the story.

It was my good fortune to live next door to the Rogers family, to know all of Phaeton's adventures, and have a part in some of them. One of the earliest was a morning canter in the country.

Phaeton was a little older than I; his brother Ned was just my age.

One day, their Uncle Jacob came to visit at their house, riding all the way from Illinois on his own horse. This horse, when he set out, was a dark bay, fourteen hands high, with one white foot, and a star on his forehead. At the first town where he staid overnight, it became an iron-gray, with a bob tail and a cast in its eye. At the next halt, the iron-gray changed into a chestnut, with two white feet and a bushy tail. A day or two afterward, he stopped at a camp-meeting, and when he left it the horse was a large roan, with just the hint of a spring-halt in its gait. Then he came to a place where a county fair was being held, and here the roan became piebald. How many more changes that horse went through, I do not know; but, when it got to us, it was about eleven hands high (convenient size for boys), nearly white, with a few black spots,—so it could be seen for a long distance, —with nice thick legs, and long hair on them to keep them warm.

For these particulars, I am indebted to Ned, who overheard the conversation between his father and his uncle, and repeated it a few times to the boys.

Now, Mr. Rogers had no barn, and his brother Jacob, who arrived in the evening, had to tie his horse in the wood-shed for the night. He might have taken it to the " Cataract House, by James Tone," which was only a short distance away, and had a first-rate stable ; but it was not the custom, in that part of the country, ever to patronize a hotel if you could by any possibility quarter yourself and your horse on a friend.

Just before bedtime, Ned came over to tell me that

Phaeton was to take the horse to pasture in the morning, that he was going with him, and they would like my company also, adding :

"Uncle Jacob says that a brisk morning canter will do us good, and give us an appetite for breakfast."

"Yes," said I, "of course it will; and besides that, we can view the scenery as we ride by."

"We can, unless we ride too fast," said Ned.

"Does your uncle's horse go very fast?" said I, with some little apprehension, for I had never been on a horse.

"I don't exactly know," said Ned. "Probably not."

"Has Phaeton ever been on a horse?" said I.

"No," said Ned; "but he is reading a book about it, that tells you just what to do."

"And how far is the pasture?"

"Four miles,—Kidd's pasture,—straight down Jay street, past the stone brewery. Kidd lives in a yellow house on the right side of the road; and when we get there we're to look out for the dog."

"It must be pretty savage, or they wouldn't tell us to look out for it. Are you going to take a pistol?"

"No; Fay says if the dog comes out, he'll ride right over him. You can't aim a pistol very steadily when you are riding full gallop on horseback."

"I suppose not," said I. "I never tried it. But after we've left the horse in the pasture, how are we to get back past the dog?"

"If Fay once rides over that dog, on that horse," said Ned, in a tone of solemn confidence, "there won't be much bite left in him when we come back."

So we said good-night, and went to bed to dream of morning canters through lovely scenery, dotted with stone breweries, and of riding triumphantly into pasture over the bodies of ferocious dogs.

A more beautiful morning never dawned, and we boys were up not much later than the sun.

The first thing to do was to untie the horse; and as he had managed to get his leg over the halter-rope, this was no easy task. Before we had accomplished it, Ned suggested that it would be better not to untie him till after we had put on the saddle; which suggestion Phaeton adopted. The saddle was pretty heavy, but we found no great difficulty in landing it on the animal's back. The trouble was, to dispose of a long strap with a loop at the end, which evidently was intended to go around the horse's tail, to keep the saddle from sliding forward upon his neck. None of us liked to try the experiment of standing behind the animal to adjust that loop.

"He looks to me like a very kicky horse," said Ned; "and I would n't like to see any of us laid up before the Fourth of July."

Phaeton thought of a good plan. Accordingly, with great labor, Ned and I assisted him to get astride the animal, with his face toward the tail, and he cautiously worked his way along the back of the now suspicious beast. But the problem was not yet solved : if he should go far enough to lift the tail and pass the strap around it, he would slide off and be kicked. Ned came to the rescue with another idea. He got a stout string, and, standing beside the animal till it happened to switch its tail around that side, caught it, and tied the string tightly to the end. Then getting to a safe distance, he proposed to pull the string and lift the tail for his brother to pass the crupper under. But as soon as he began to pull, the horse began to kick ; and not only to kick, but to rear, bumping Phaeton's head against the roof of the low shed, so that he was obliged to lie flat and hang on tight. While this was going on, their Uncle Jacob appeared, and asked what they were doing.

"Putting on the saddle, sir," said I.

"Yes, it looks like it," said he. "But I did n't intend to have you take the saddle."

"Why not, uncle?" said Phaeton.

"Because it is too heavy for you to bring back."

"Oh, but we can leave it there," said Phaeton. "Hang it up in Kidd's barn."

"No ; that won't do," said his uncle. "Can't tell who might use it or abuse it. I'll strap on a blanket, and you can ride just as well on that."

"But none of us have been used to riding that way," said Ned.

Without replying, his uncle folded a blanket, laid it on the horse's back, and fastened it with a surcingle. He then bridled and led out the animal.

"Who rides first?" said he.

I was a little disappointed at this, for I had supposed that we should all ride at once. Still, I was comforted that he had not merely said, "Who rides?"—but "Who rides first?"—implying that we were all to ride in turn. Phaeton stepped forward, and his uncle lifted him upon the horse, and put the bridle-reins into his hand.

"I think you wont need any whip," said he, as he turned and went into the house.

The horse walked slowly down till he came to a full stop, with his breast against the front gate.

"Open the gate, Ned," said Phaeton..

"I can't do it, unless you back him," answered Ned. This was true, for the gate opened inward.

"Back, Dobbin!" said Phaeton, in a stern voice of authority, giving a vigorous jerk upon the reins.

But Dobbin did n't back an inch.

"Why don't you back him?" said Ned, as if it were the easiest thing in the world.

"Why don't you open that gate?" said Phaeton.

By this time, three or four boys had gathered on the sidewalk, and were staring at our performance.

"Shall I hit him?" said Ned, breaking a switch.

" No," said Phaeton, more excited than before;
"don't touch him! Back, Dobbin! Back!"

But Dobbin seemed to be one of those heroic characters who take no step backward.

" I know how to manage it," said Ned, as he ran to
the wood-pile and selected a small round stick. Thrusting the end of this under the gate, he pried it up until he
had lifted it from its hinges, when it fell over outward,
coming down with a tremendous slam-bang upon the
sidewalk. A great shiver ran through Dobbin, beginning
at the tips of his ears, and ending at his shaggy fetlocks.
Then, with a quick snort, he made a wild bound over the
prostrate gate, and landed in the middle of the road.

I don't know how Phaeton managed to keep his seat,
but he did ; and though the boys on the sidewalk set up
a shout, Dobbin stood perfectly still in the road, waiting
for the next earthquake, or falling gate, or something, to
give him another start.

"Come on, boys! Never mind the gate!" said Phaeton.

When he said " boys," he only meant Ned and me.
But the boys on the sidewalk promptly accepted the invitation and came on, too.

"You walk on the nigh side," said Phaeton to me,
" and let Ned take the off side."

I was rather puzzled as to his exact meaning ; and yet
I was proud to think that the boy who represented what

might now be considered our party on horseback, as distinguished from the strangers on foot crowding alongside; was able to use a few technical terms. Not wishing to display my ignorance, I loitered a little, to leave the choice of sides to Ned, confident that he would know which was nigh and which was off. He promptly placed himself on the left side, near enough to seize his brother by the left leg, if need be, and either hold him on or pull him off. I, of course, then took a similar position on the right side.

" He told you to take the nigh side," shouted one of the boys to me.

" He's all right," said Phaeton. " I'd advise you to hurry home before your breakfast gets cold. We'll run this horse without any more help."

" Run him, will you ?" answered the boy derisively. " That's what I'm waiting to see. He'll run so fast the grass 'll grow under his feet."

" If there was a hot breakfast an inch ahead of your nose," said another of the boys, addressing Phaeton, " it 'd be stone cold before you got to it."

Notwithstanding these sarcastic remarks, our horse was now perceptibly moving. He had begun to walk along in the middle of the road, and—what at the time seemed to me very fortunate—he was going in the direction of the pasture.

" Can't you make him go faster, Fay ?" said Ned.

I*

"Not in this condition," said Phaeton. "You can't expect a horse without a saddle on him to make very good time."

"What difference does that make?" said I.

"You read the book, and you'll see," said Phaeton, in that tone of superior information which is common to people who have but just learned what they are talking about, and not learned it very well. "All the directions in the book are for horses with saddles on them. There is n't one place where it tells about a horse with just a blanket strapped over his back. If Uncle Jacob had let me take the saddle, and if I had a good pair of wheel-spurs, and a riding-whip, and a gag-bit in his mouth, you would n't see me here. By this time I should be just a little cloud of dust, away up there beyond the brew-ery. This animal shows marks of speed, and I'll bet you, if he was properly handled, he'd trot way down in the thirties."

So much good horse-talk, right out of a standard book, rather awed me. But I ventured to suggest that I could cut him a switch from the hedge, which Dobbin could certainly be made to feel, though it might not be so elegant as a riding-whip.

"Never mind it," said he. "It's no use; you can't expect much of any horse without saddle or spurs. And besides, what would become of you and Ned? You could n't keep up."

I suggested that he might go on a mile or two and then return to meet us, and so have all the more ride. But he answered : " I'm afraid Uncle Jacob would n't like that. He expects us to go right to the pasture, without delay. You just wait till I get a good saddle, with Mexican stirrups, and wheel-spurs."

By this time, the boys who had been following us had dropped off. But at the next corner three or four others espied us, and gathered around.

" Why don't you make him go ? " said one who had a switch in his hand, with which at the same time he gave Dobbin a smart blow on the flank.

A sort of shiver of surprise ran through Dobbin. Then he planted his fore feet firmly and evenly on the ground, as if he had been told to toe a mark, and threw out his hind ones, so that for an instant they formed a continuous straight line with his body. The boy who had struck him, standing almost behind him, narrowly escaped being sent home to his breakfast with no appetite at all.

" Lick those fellows ! " said Phaeton to Ned and me, as he leaned over Dobbin's neck and seized his mane with a desperate grip.

" There are too many of them," said Ned.

" Well, lick the curly-headed one, any way," said Phaeton, " if he does n't know better than to hit a horse with a switch."

Ned started for him, and the boy, diving through an open gate and dodging around a small barn, was last seen going over two or three back fences, with Ned all the while just one fence behind him.

When they were out of sight, the remaining boys turned their attention again to Dobbin, and one of them threw a pebble, which hit him on the nose and made him perform very much as before, excepting that this time he planted his hind feet and threw his fore feet into the air.

" Go for that fellow ! " said Phaeton to me.

He struck off in a direction opposite to that taken by the curly-headed boy, and I followed him. It was a pretty rough chase that he led me ; but he seemed to know every step of the way, and when he ran into the culvert by which the Deep Hollow stream passed under the canal, I gave it up, and made my way back. That he should have run from me, seemed at first a mystery, for he had a far better pugilistic record than I. But he probably ran because he was conscious of being in the wrong, as he had no shadow of right to throw a pebble at the nose of another boy's horse. This proves the power of a just cause.

Calculating that Phaeton must have passed on some distance by this time, I took a diagonal path across a field, and struck into the road near the stone brewery. Phaeton had not yet arrived, and I sat down in the shade of the building. Presently, Dobbin came up the road at a jog trot, with Phaeton wobbling around on his back, like a ball in a fountain. The cause of his speed was the clatter of an empty barrel-rack being driven along behind him.

On arriving at the brewery, he turned and, in spite of Phaeton's frantic " Whoas !" and rein-jerking, went right through a low-arched door, scraping off his rider as he passed in.

" So much for not having a gag-bit," said Phaeton, as he picked himself up. " I remember, Uncle Jacob said the horse had worked fifteen or sixteen years in a brewery. That was a long time ago, but it seems he has n't forgotten it yet. And now I don't suppose we can ever get him out of there without a gag-bit."

He had hardly said this, however, when one of the brewery men came leading out Dobbin. Then the inquiry was for Ned, who had not been seen since he went over the third fence after the curly-headed boy who did n't know any better than to hit a horse with a switch. Phaeton decided that we must wait for him. In about fifteen minutes, one of the great brewery wagons came up the road, and as it turned in at the gate, Ned dropped from the hind axle, where he had been catching a ride.

After we had exchanged the stories of our adventures, Ned said it was now his turn to ride.

" I wish you could, Ned," said Phaeton ; " but I don't

dare trust you on his back. He's too fiery and untamable. It's all _I_ can do to hold him."

Ned grumbled somewhat; but with the help of the brewery man, Phaeton remounted, and we set off again for Kidd's pasture. Ned and I walked close beside the horse, each with the fingers of one hand between his body and the surcingle, that we might either hold him or be taken along with him if he should again prove fiery and untamable.

When we got to the canal bridge, we found that a single plank was missing from the road-way. Nothing could induce Dobbin to step across that open space. All sorts of coaxing and argument were used, and even a few gentle digs from Phaeton's heels, but it was of no avail. At last he began to back, and Ned and I let go of the surcingle. Around he wheeled, and down the steep bank he went, like the picture of Putnam at Horseneck, landed on the tow-path, and immediately plunged into the water. A crowd of boys who were swimming under the bridge set up a shout, as he swam across with Phaeton on his back, and, climbing out on the other side, accompanied us along the road as far as the requirements of civilization would permit.

Ned and I crossed by the bridge.

"I only hope Uncle Jacob won't blame me if the horse takes cold," said Phaeton.

"Can't we prevent it?" said Ned.

" What can you do ? " said Phaeton.

" I think we ought to rub him off perfectly dry, at once," said Ned. " That's the way Mr. Gifford's groom does."

" I guess that's so," said Phaeton. " You two go to that hay-stack over there, and get some good wisps to rub him down."

Ned and I each brought a large armful of hay.

" Now, see here, Fay," said Ned, " you've got to get off from that horse and help rub him. We're not going to do it all."

" But how can I get on again ? " said Phaeton.

" I don't care how," said Ned. " You've had all the ride, and you must expect to do some of the work. If you don't, I'll let him die of quick consumption before I'll rub him."

This vigorous declaration of independence had a good effect. Phaeton slid down, and tied Dobbin to the fence, and we all set to work and used up the entire supply of hay in rubbing him dry.

After several unsuccessful attempts to mount him by bringing him close to the fence, Phaeton determined to lead him the rest of the way.

" Anyhow, I suppose he ought not to have too violent exercise after such a soaking as that," said he. " We'll let him rest a little."

As we were now beyond the limits of the town, the

only spectators were individual boys and girls, who were generally swinging on farm-yard gates. Most of these, however, took interest enough to inquire why we did n't ride. We paid no attention to their suggestions, but walked quietly along,—Phaeton at the halter, and Ned and I at the sides,—as if guarding the sacred bull of Burmah.

About a mile of this brought us to Mr. Kidd's.

" What about riding over the dog?" said Ned.

" We can't very well ride over him to-day, when we've neither saddle nor spurs," said Phaeton; "but you two might get some good stones, and be ready for him."

Accordingly we two selected some good stones. Ned crowded one into each of his four pockets, and carried one in each hand. I contented myself with two in my hands.

" There's no need of getting so many," said Phaeton. " For if you don't hit him the first time, he'll be on you before you can throw another."

This was not very comforting; but we kept on, and Ned said it would n't do any harm to have plenty of ammunition. When we reached the house, there was no dog in sight, excepting a small shaggy one asleep on the front steps.

" You hold Dobbin," said Phaeton to me, " while I go in and make arrangements."

I think I held Dobbin about half a minute, at the end of which time he espied an open gate at the head of a long lane leading to the pasture, jerked the halter from my hand, and trotted off at surprising speed. When Phaeton came out of the house, of course I told him what had happened.

" But it's just as well," said I, " for he has gone right down to the pasture."

" No, it is n't just as well," said he ; " we must get off the halter and blanket."

" But what about the dog ? " said Ned.

" Oh, that one on the steps won't hurt anybody. The savage one is down in the wood-lot."

At this moment a woman appeared at the side door of the farm-house, looked out at us, and understood the whole situation in a moment.

" I suppose you had n't watered your horse," said she, " and he's gone for the creek."

Phaeton led the way to the pasture, and we followed. I should n't like to tell you how very long we chased Dobbin around that lot, trying to corner him. We tried swift running, and we tried slow approaches. I suggested salt. Ned pretended to fill his hat with oats, and walked up with coaxing words. But Dobbin knew the difference between a straw hat and a peck measure.

" I wish I could remember what the book says about catching your horse," said Phaeton.

" I wish you could," said I. " Why did n't you bring the book ? "

"I will next time," said he, as he started off in another desperate attempt to corner the horse between the creek and the fence.

Nobody can tell how long this might have kept up, had not an immense black dog appeared, jumping over the fence from the wood-lot.

Phaeton drew back and looked about for a stone. Ned began tugging at one of those in his pockets, but could n't get it out. Instead of coming at us, the dog made straight for Dobbin, soon reached him, seized the halter in his teeth, and brought him to a full stop, where he held him till we came up. It only took a minute or two to remove the blanket and halter, and turn Dobbin loose, while a few pats on the head and words of praise made a fast friend of the dog.

With these trappings over our arms, we turned our steps homeward. As we drew near the place where we had given Dobbin the rubbing down to keep him from taking cold, we saw a man looking over the fence at the wet wisps of hay in the road.

"I wonder if that man will expect us to pay for the hay," said Phaeton.

"It would be just like him," said Ned. "These farmers are an awful stingy set."

"I have n't got any money with me," said Phaeton; "but I know a short cut home."

Ned and I agreed that any shortening of the homeward journey would be desirable just now,—especially as we were very hungry.

He led the way, which required him to go back to the first cross-road, and we followed. It seemed to me that the short cut home was about twice as long as the road by which we had come, but as I also was oppressed with a sense of having no money with me, I sympathized with Phaeton, and made no objection. When I found that the short cut led through the Deep Hollow culvert, I confess to some vague fears that the boy I had chased into the culvert might dam up the water while we were in there, or play some other unpleasant trick on us, and I was glad when we were well through it with only wet feet and shoulders spattered by the drippings from the arch.

We got home at last, and Phaeton told his uncle that Dobbin was safe in the pasture, at the same time giving him to understand that we were—as we always say at the end of a composition—much pleased with our brisk morning canter. But the boys could n't help talking about it, and gradually the family learned every incident of the story. When Mr. Rogers heard about the hay, he sent Phaeton with some money to pay for it, but the stingy farmer said it was no matter, and would n't take any pay. But he asked Phaeton where we were going, and told him he had a pasture that was just as good as Kidd's, and nearer the town.

CHAPTER II.

IF Phaeton Rogers was not an immediate success as a rider of horses, he certainly did what seemed some wonderful things in the way of inventing conveyances for himself and other people to ride.

One day, not long after our adventures with Dobbin, Ned and I found him sitting under the great plane-tree in the front yard, working with a knife at some small pieces of wood, which he put together, making a frame like this:

"What are you making, Fay?" said Ned.

"An invention," said Phaeton, without looking up from his work.

"What sort of invention? A new invention?"

"It would have to be new or it would n't be an invention at all."

"But what is it for?"

"For the benefit of mankind, like all great inventions."

"It seems to me that some of the best have been for the benefit of boykind," said Ned. "But what is the use of trying to be too smart? Let us know what it is. We're not likely to steal it, as Lem Woodruff thinks the patent-lawyer stole his idea for a double-acting washboard."

Phaeton was silent, and worked away. Ned and I walked out at the gate and turned into the street, intending to go swimming. We had not gone far when Phaeton called "Ned!" and we turned back.

"Ned," said he, "don't you want to lend me the ten dollars that Aunt Mercy gave you last week?"

Their Aunt Mercy was an unmarried lady with considerable property, who was particularly good to Ned. When Phaeton was a baby she wanted to name him after the man who was to have been her husband, but who was drowned at sea.

Mrs. Rogers would not consent, but insisted upon naming the boy Fayette, and Aunt Mercy had never liked him, and would never give him anything, or believe that he could do anything good or creditable. She was a little deaf, and if it was told her that Phaeton had taken a prize at school, she pretended not to hear; but whenever Ned got one she had no trouble at all in hearing about it, and she always gave him at least a dollar or

two on such occasions.   For when Ned was born she was
allowed to do what she had wanted to do with Fayette,
and named him Edmund Burton, after her long-lost
lover.   Later, she impressed it upon him that he was
never to write his name E. B. Rogers, nor Edmund B.
Rogers, but always Edmund Burton Rogers, if he wanted
to please her, and be remembered in her will.   She never
called him anything but Edmund Burton.   Whereas, she
pretended not to remember Fayette's name at all, and
would twist it in all sorts of ways, calling him Layit and
Brayit, and Fater and Faylen, and once she called him
Frenchman-what's-his-name, which was as near as she
ever came to getting it right.

"Why should I lend you my ten dollars?" said Ned.
"For the information you kindly gave us about your invention?"

"Oh, as to that," said Phaeton, "I've no objection to
telling you two about it, now that I have thought it all
out.   I did not care to tell you before, because I was
studying on it."

"All right; go ahead," said Ned, as we seated ourselves on the grass, and Phaeton began.

"It is called the Underground Railway.   You see,
there are some places—like the city of New York, for
instance—where the buildings are so close together, and
land is worth so much, that they can't build railroads
enough to carry all the people back and forth.   And so

they have been trying, in all sorts of ways, to get up something that will do it—something different from a common railroad."

"Balloons would be the thing," said Ned.

"No; balloons wont do," said Phaeton. "You can't make them 'light where you want them to. I've thought of a good many ways, but there was some fault in all of them but this last one."

"Tell us about the others first," said Ned.

"I'll show you *one* of them," said Phaeton, and he drew from his pocket a small sheet of paper, which he unfolded.

"This," said he, "represents the city of New York. *A* is some place far up-town where people live; *B* is the Battery, which is down-town where they do the business. I suppose you both know what a mortar is?"

"A cannon as big around as it is long," said Ned.

"And shoots bomb-shells," said I.

"That's it," said Phaeton. "Now here, you see, is a big mortar up-town; only, instead of shooting a bomb-shell,

it shoots a car. This car has no wheels, and has a big knob of India-rubber on the end for a buffer. When you get it full of people, you lock it up tight and touch off the mortar. This dotted mark represents what is called the line of flight. You see, it comes down into another sort of mortar, which has a big coiled spring inside, to stop it easy and prevent it from smashing. Then the depot-master puts up a long step-ladder and lets the people out."

Ned said he should like to be the one to touch off the mortar.

"And why was n't that a good plan?" said I.

"There are some serious objections to it," said Phaeton, in a knowing way, "For instance, you can't aim such a thing very true when the wind is blowing hard, and people might not like to ride in it on a windy day. Besides, some people have a very strong prejudice, you know, against any sort of fire-arms."

"There would n't be much chance for a boy to catch a ride on it," said Ned, as if that were the most serious objection of all. "But tell us about the real invention."

"The real invention," said Phaeton, "is this," and he took up the little frame we had seen him making. Taking an India-rubber string from his pocket, he stretched it from one of the little posts to the other, and fastened it.

"Now," said he, "suppose there was a fly that lived

up at this end, and had his office down at that end. He gets his breakfast, and takes his seat right here," and he laid his finger on the string, near one of the posts. " I call out, ' All aboard ! ' and then——"

Here Phaeton, who had his knife in his hand, cut the string in two behind the imaginary fly.

" Where is the fly now ? " said he. " At his office doing business—"

" I don't understand," said Ned.

" I've only half explained it," said Phaeton. " Now, you see, it's easy enough to make a tunnel under-ground and run cars through. But a tunnel always gets full of smoke when a train goes through, which is very disagree-able, and if you send a train every fifteen minutes, all the passengers would choke. So, you see, there must be something instead of an engine and a train of cars. I propose to dig a good tunnel wherever the road wants to go, and make it as long as you please. Right through the centre I pass an India-rubber cable as large as a man's leg, and stretch it tight and fasten it to great posts at each end. All the men and boys who want to go sit on at one end, as if on horseback. When everything is ready, the train-despatcher takes a sharp axe, and with one blow clips the cable in two behind them, and zip they go to the other end before you can say Jack Robinson."

Ned said he should like to be train-despatcher.

" They'd all have to hang on like time," said I.

2

"Of course they would," said Phaeton ; "but there are little straps for them to take hold by."

"And would there be a tub at the other end," said Ned "to catch the passengers that were broken to pieces against the end wall ? "

"Oh, pshaw ! " said Phaeton.   "Don't you suppose I have provided for that ? "

The fact was, Phaeton had spent more study on the question of landing his passengers safely than on any other part of his invention.   It was not the first instance since the days of the hand-mill that made the sea salt, in which it had been found easy to set a thing going, but difficult to stop it.

"There are several ways," said he, continuing his explanation, "to let the passengers off safely.   I have n't decided yet what I'll adopt.   One way is, to have a sort of brake to squeeze down on the cable and make it stop gradually.   I don't exactly like that, because it would wear out the cable, and these cables are going to cost a great deal of money.   Another way is, to throw them against a big, soft mattress, like pins in a bowling-alley. But even that would hurt a little, I guess, no matter how soft you made the mattress.   The best way is, to have it drop them in a tank of water."

"What ! and get all wet ? " said Ned.

"Don't be in a hurry," said Phaeton.   "Each one would wear an India-rubber water-proof garment (a sort

of over-dress), covering him all over and fastened up
tight. Of course, these would be provided by the company."

" But would n't it use up a cable every time you cut
it ? " said Ned.

" Not at all ; it could be stretched again by hitching a
team of horses to the end and drawing it back, and then
we should solder it together with melted India-rubber.
Probably a dozen teams would be at work at night
stretching cables for use next day. You see, we should
have as many cables as the business of the road required."

I have never known whether Phaeton was sincere in
all this, or whether he was simply fooling Ned and me.
I have since suspected that he had a purpose which did
not appear at the time. At any rate, we took it all in
and believed it all, and looked upon him as one of the
world's great inventors.

" And what do you want the ten dollars for ? " said
Ned.

" Well, you know nothing can be done without more
or less money," said Phaeton. " The first thing is, to
get up a model to send to the Patent-Office, and get a
patent on it."

" What's that ? " said Ned.

" What's what ? "

" A model."

"A model," said Phaeton, "is a little one, with tunnel and all complete, to show how it works."

"But a tunnel," said Ned, "is a hole in the ground. You can't send a hole in the ground to the Patent-Office, no matter how small you make it."

"Oh, pshaw! Don't you understand? There would be a little wooden tube or shell, painted red, to represent the brick-work that the real tunnel would be arched in with."

"Well, what then?"

"I suppose it would cost about ten dollars to get up a model. If it's going to the Patent-Office it does n't want to be botched up with a pocket-knife."

"Of course not," said Ned. "But the model will be only a beginning. It will take a great deal more money than that to build the real thing."

"Now you talk business," said Phaeton. "And I'm ready to talk with you. I've thought it all out. I got an idea from the way that Father says Mr. Drake manages to build so many houses."

"Let's hear about it."

"There are two ways to get the thing into operation. One is, to try it first in this town. You know we boys could dig the tunnel ourselves, and it would n't cost anything."

"Yes, I suppose so—if enough boys would take hold."

"Then we could give a mortgage on the tunnel, and so raise money to buy the cable, and there you are."

"That's all very fine," said Ned ; "but they foreclose mortgages. And if there was a mortgage on our tunnel, and they foreclosed it while we were in there, what would become of us ? How should we ever get out ?"

Phaeton laughed.

"I'll tell you how we'll fix it," said he. "We'll have a secret shaft leading out of the tunnel, and not let the man we give the mortgage to know anything about it."

Ned did n't exactly know whether he was being quizzed or not.

"What's the other way of getting the thing into operation ?" said he.

"The other way," said Phaeton, "is to go to New York and see Uncle Silas, and have him get up a company to start it there."

"I think I like that way best," said Ned. "But, to tell you the truth, I had made arrangements to do something else with that ten dollars."

Phaeton looked disappointed.

"Then why did n't you say so in the first place ?" said he, as he put his things into his pocket and turned to walk away.

"Don't get mad, Fay," said Ned. "Perhaps we can get another ten."

"Where can we get it ?"

"Of Aunt Mercy."

"You might, but I can't."

"Well, I'll try to get it for you, if you'll let me take your machine."

"All right," said Phaeton. "When will you go?"

"I might as well go this evening as any time," said Ned.

So it was agreed that he should visit his Aunt Mercy that evening, and see if she would advance the money for a model. I was to go with him, but Phaeton was to be kept entirely in the background.

"Do you suppose Fay can really make anything out of this machine?" said Ned to me, as we were on the way to his Aunt Mercy's.

"I should think he might," said I. "For he is certainly a genius, and he seems to have great faith in it."

"At any rate, we might as well get fifteen dollars while we are about it," said Ned.

"I suppose we might," said I.

CHAPTER III.

AUNT MERCY.

"Good evening, Aunty."

"Good evening, Edmund Burton."

Aunt Mercy was sipping a cup of tea, and reading the evening paper.

"What's the news, Aunty?"

"Another railroad accident, of course."

"Nobody hurt, I hope?"

"Yes; a great many. I wonder that anybody's fool-hardy enough to ride on the railroads."

"How did it happen?" said Ned, beginning to think it was a poor time to get money for a railroad invention.

"Train ran off the track," said Aunt Mercy, "and ran right down an embankment. Seems to me they always do. I don't see why they have so many embankments."

"They ought not to," said Ned. "If they only knew it, there's a way to make a railroad without any track, or any wheels to run off the track, or any embankment to run down if they did run off."

"You don't say so, Edmund Burton! What sort of a railroad would that be?"

" I happen to have the plan of one with me," said Ned.

" E d m u n d B u r t o n ! What *do* you mean ? "

" I mean this," said Ned, pulling from his pocket the little frame with a rubber string stretched on it. " It's a new invention ; has n't been patented yet."

" E d m u n d B u r t o n ! " was all his aunt could say.

" I'll explain it to you, Aunty," said Ned, as he picked up the newspaper which she had dropped, and rolled it into a tube.

" This," said he, " represents a tunnel, a big round hole, you know, as big as this room, bored along in the ground. It goes right through rocks and everything, and is perfectly straight. No dangerous curves. And this " —showing the frame and then passing it into the paper tube —" represents an India-rubber cable as large as a stove-pipe. It is stretched out as far as possible, and fastened tight to posts at the ends."

" E d m u n d B u r t o n ! "

" Now, Aunty, we'll call this end Albany, and this end Buffalo."   ·

" E d m u n d B u r t o n ! "

" All the men and boys in Albany that want to go to Buffalo could come down to the depot, and get on the cable right there, sitting just as if they were on horseback, and there will be nice little straps for them to hold on by."

"Edmund Burton!"

"When everybody's ready, the train-despatcher just picks up a sharp axe, and with one blow cuts the cable in two, right here, and zip! the passengers find themselves in Buffalo. No boiler to burst, no track to get off from, no embankment to plunge down, no wheels to get out of order."

"Edmund Burton, you *are* a genius! But ladies can't ride that way."

"Of course not," said Ned, catching an idea. "We have a car for the ladies. This"—and he picked up a spool of thread and a lead pencil, and passed the pencil through the spool—"represents it. The pencil represents the cable, and the spool represents the car, which is fastened tight on the cable. When the ladies are all in, it is locked up, and then the cable is cut behind it."

"Edmund Burton!"

"And the great advantage of it is, that the car is perfectly round, and so whichever way it might happen to turn, it would always be right side up, for every side is the right side!"

"Edmund Burton, you *are* a genius!"

"But you mustn't tell anybody about it, Aunty, for it hasn't been patented yet."

"Why don't you patent it, Edmund Burton?"

"We think of doing so, Aunty, but it will cost more money than we have just now. The first thing is to get up a model."

2*

" What's that, Edmund Burton ? "

" A little one, with tunnel and everything complete, to show how it works. That has to go to the Patent-Office and be put in a glass case."

" And how much will it cost to make a muddle, Edmund Burton ? "

" Fay says he thinks one *could* be made for ten dollars ; but I suppose more money would build a better one."

" Your brother knows nothing about it, Edmund Burton. *He* would get up a miserable cheap muddle, and disgrace the family. Don't let him have anything to do with it. Jane ! "—calling to the servant—" bring me my pocket-book from the right-hand corner of my top bureau drawer."

Jane brought it.

" How much will it take for a good muddle, Edmund Burton ? " said his Aunt Mercy, as she opened her pocket-book.

" I should think fifteen dollars ought to be a great plenty," said Ned, and she handed him a crisp new ten-dollar bill and a five.

" Thank you, Aunty."

" You're welcome, child. Always come to me when you want money to make a muddle. But mind what I tell you, Edmund Burton. Don't let that numskull brother of yours have anything to do with it, and be sure you get up a handsome muddle that will do credit to the family."

"Yes, Aunty. Good-night!"

"Good-night! But come and kiss me before you go, Edmund Burton."

"Don't you think," said Ned, as we were walking home, "before Fay goes any further with this invention, and spends money on it, he'd better talk with somebody who knows more about such things than we do?"

I did n't quite know whether Ned said this because he was really anxious about the fate of the invention, or because he did not like to part with the money, now that he actually had it. Some people are always ready to say that they would lend money to a friend, if they had it; but when they feel it in their hands, they are not in such a hurry to let it go out. However, I thought this was a good idea, whatever might be Ned's reason for suggesting it; so I said, "Certainly, he ought! Who do you think would be the best person for him to talk with?"

"I don't know anybody better than Jack-in-the-Box," said Ned. "Of course he knows all about railroads."

"Of course he does," said I, "and he'll be glad to help us. Jack-in-the-Box is the very one!"

CHAPTER IV.

JACK-IN-THE-BOX.

THE box was a red box, about five feet square and eight feet high, with a pointed top. Jack was about five feet nine inches high, with a brown beard and mustache and dark hazel eyes, and might have been twenty-six years old, possibly older. When he was in the box, he wore a blue blouse and dark trousers and a small cloth cap. The only time I ever saw him away from the box was on Sundays, when he always came to the Presbyterian Church, and sat in pew No. 79. One of the great pillars that supported the gallery was planted in this pew, and spoiled nearly the whole of it; but there was a comfortable seat for one at the outer end, and Jack had that seat. The box had two small square windows on opposite sides. On another side was a door, with 248 over it. The fourth side was covered in summer with morning-glory vines, planted by Jack, and trained to run up on strings. A stove-pipe about as large as your arm stuck out at the top. When Jack looked out at one of his windows, he looked up the railroad; when he looked out at the other, he looked down the railroad; when he stepped out of his door, he stood beside the track, and on those occasions he generally had in his hand either a red flag or a red lantern.

Close beside the box rose a tall, heavy pole, with a cross-piece on the top and short iron rods stuck through it at intervals all the way up. A rope passed over pulleys in the ends of the cross-piece, and Jack used to hoist sometimes three white balls, sometimes two red balls, at night tying on white or red lanterns below the balls.

To us boys, Jack was a delightful character, in an enviable situation, but to older people he was a mystery. I remember one day I was walking with Father, when Mr. Briggs joined us, and as we came in sight of the box, Jack was rolling up his flag, a train having just gone by.

"What do you make of that young man?" said Mr. Briggs.

"I don't know what to make of him," said Father. "He is evidently not the sort of man they generally have in those positions. You can tell by his speech and manner, and his whole appearance, that he is an educated man and a gentleman."

"Oh, yes," said Mr. Briggs. "If you peep in at the window, you will see a shelf full of books. He seems to have taken this way to make a hermit of himself—not a bad way, either, in these modern times, when there are no uninhabited wilds to retire to, and when a little money income is absolutely necessary to existence."

"I should like to know his history," said Father.

"Either he has committed some crime—forgery, perhaps—and escaped," said Mr. Briggs, "or he has quarrelled with his family, or in some way been disappointed."

"I don't think it's for any crime," said Father; "his appearance forbids that."

"Still, you can't always tell," said Mr. Briggs. "I tried to make his acquaintance once, but did not succeed. I am told he repels all advances. Even the Presbyterian minister, whose church he attends, can't get at him."

"I understand he likes the boys, and makes their acquaintance," said Father.

We had now arrived at our gate, and Mr. Briggs said good evening, and passed on.

It was true that Jack-in-the-Box was partial to boys; in fact, nobody else could make his acquaintance. He liked to have us come and talk with him, but never wanted more than two or three to come at a time. Perhaps this was on account of the size of the box. We used to consult him on all sorts of occasions, and got a great many shrewd hints and useful bits of information from him.

The inside of the box was a romance to me. I never saw so many things in so small a space. In one corner was a stove about as large as a coffee-pot, and beside it a sheet-iron coal-box, not much larger. In another corner stood the red flag, when it was furled, and a hatchet.

Behind the door, hung flat on the wall, was a large coil of rope. Overhead, on one side, was a shelf, nearly filled with tools and trinkets. On the opposite side—lower, but still over the window—was another shelf, filled with books. I took a special interest in this shelf, and studied the backs of the books so often, that I think I can give the title of every one, in their order. They were, beginning at the left hand, a Bible, "Essays of Elia," "Henry Esmond," "Life of Columbus," "Twice-told Tales," "Anatomy of Melancholy," "Modern Painters," "The Shadows of the Clouds," "The Middle Ages," "Undine and Sintram," "Tales of the Great St. Bernard," "Sordello," "Divina Commedia," "Sophoclis Tragœdiæ," "Demosthenis Orationes," "Platonis Dialogi," "Q. Horatii Flacci Opera," "Robinson Crusoe," "Byron's Poems," and Shakespeare. I was so curious about them, that I copied off all the hard ones on a card, and, when I went home, tried to find out what they were.

Under the book-shelf, at one side of the window, fastened to the wall, was a little alarm-clock. Jack knew exactly what time every train would come along. As soon as one had passed, and he had rolled up his flag, he used to set the alarm so that it would go off two minutes before the next train was due. Then he could sit down with his book, and be sure of not forgetting his duty.

Jack generally sat in a sort of easy chair with one arm to it, on which a board was fastened in such a way as to

make a little writing-desk. The space under the seat of
the chair was boxed, with a little door on one side, and in
there he kept his stationery.

Hardly a day passed that Jack did not have boy
visitors. There were only two things about him that
seemed singular to me. We could never find out his real
name. He told us to call him simply Jack ; whereupon
Isaac Holman said the full name must be Jack-in-the-Box,
and after that we always called him by the full name.
The other queer thing was, that he was never known to
read a newspaper. The boys sometimes brought one to
him, but he always said he did n't care about it, and would
not open it. Father and Mr. Briggs appeared to think it
very strange that he should live in that box and attend to
the flags and signals. To me it seemed the most delightful
life imaginable, and Jack-in-the-Box was one of my heroes.
I often thought that if I could choose my own station in
life, my choice would be a flag-station on the railroad.

Phaeton adopted Ned's suggestion as to consulting
Jack-in-the-Box about his invention, and we three went
together to see him.

When we got there, the door of the box stood wide
open ; everything seemed to be in its place, but Jack
had disappeared.

" Probably gone up the road, to flag an extra train,"
said Phaeton. " No, he has n't, for there's his flag in its
place in the corner."

"He can't have been murdered," said Ned, "or they would have robbed the box. Must be suicide. Perhaps we'd better take charge of his things."

"I would n't be in a hurry about that," said Phaeton.

"Or he may have been run over by a train that he did n't see," said Ned, getting excited, and examining the rails in search of blood-marks. "If he was trying to remember all that funny-looking Greek stuff in some of those books, I should n't think he would notice a train, or anything else. And we'll all have to sit on the coroner's jury. Poor Jack! I don't believe we can say the train was to blame, or make it pay damages. I think I should like to sit near the feet; for he had handsome feet and only wore number six boots. He was an awful good fellow, too. But that 'll take us out of school one day, anyway."

"So you think there is no great loss without some small gain," said Phaeton.

"I did n't say so!" said Ned, a little offended at this plain interpretation of his last sentence. "I feel as badly as anybody about Jack's death. But, at any rate, they'll have to do something with his property. I suppose, if he had no relations—and I never heard of any—they'll give it to his best friends. I think I should like the alarm-clock, and the chair, and perhaps a few of the tools. What will you take?" turning to me.

"I think I should like to take his place, if anything," said I.

Ned took a look at the box.

"I tell you what it is," said he, "the prettiest design for a monument over Jack's grave would be a box just like that—all cut in marble, of course—with Jack's name and age on the door, and beside it a signal-pole struck by lightning and broken off in the middle, or something of that sort."

A slight noise, or else the allusion to the signal-pole, caused us to look up. There was Jack coming down, with an oil-can in his hand! He had been at the top oiling the pulleys, and had probably heard every word we said, for there was a quiet smile all over his face.

"Good morning, Jack," said Phaeton, who seldom lost his presence of mind.

"Good morning, boys. I'm glad to see you," said Jack.

As soon as Ned and I could recover from our abashment, we also said good morning.

"Is there anything I can do for you to-day?" said Jack, as he set away the oil-can, observing that Phaeton had the little frame and a small drawing in his hand.

"Yes, sir," said Phaeton. "I want to get your advice about a little invention that I've been making."

"It's a new kind of railroad," said Ned; "and we thought you'd be the one to know all about railroads. Beats these common railroads all to nothing. Why, three months after ours is introduced, and the public under-

THE BOYS CONSULT JACK-IN-THE-BOX.

stand it, they'll have to take up this track and sell it for old iron."

Ned had thoroughly identified himself with the invention, and thought it was as much his as Phaeton's.

"But then," he added thoughtfully, " that would spoil your business, Jack. And we should be sorry to do that."

Jack smiled, and said it did n't matter ; he would n't wish to let his private interests obstruct the march of improvement.

Phaeton explained the invention to Jack, illustrating it with a rubber-string stretched on the frame, just as he had explained it to us.

"I see," said Jack. "Quite a novel idea."

"We have n't made up our minds," said Ned, "what sort of depot we'll have. But it 'll be either a big tank full of water, or an awful soft mattress."

"How is that ?" said Jack.

"Why, you see," said Ned, "this railroad of ours is going to go like lightning. There's no trouble about its going."

"None whatever," said Jack.

"But it's going to stop rather sudden."

"How so ?" said Jack.

"I mean the trains," said Ned. "That is, the cables. They're going to fetch up with a bang at the other end. At least, they would, if we had n't thought

of a way to prevent it.   Because it would n't do to break
the heads of all the passengers every time."

"No," said Jack.   "That would be too much."

"Too much," said Ned.   "And so you see the depot
must be some sort of contrivance to let 'em off easy."

"Of course," said Jack.

"And the first thing anybody thinks of is a bowling-
alley, and the pins flying every which way."

"Quite naturally," said Jack.

"And that makes you think of a soft mattress to stop
them.   But Fay thinks it would be better, on some
accounts, to drop them into a big tank of water."

"I suppose in winter you would have the water
warmed?" said Jack.

"Of course we should; though we had n't thought of
it before," said Ned.

"And that would give the passengers a ride and a
bath, all for the price of one ticket," said Jack.

"Certainly; and you see that would be favorable to
the poor," said Ned, willing to indulge in the joke.

"Exactly; a great boon to mankind," said Jack.
"And I think it would not only make them cleaner, but
more religious."

"How so?" said Ned.

"Well, I think every passenger would feel like saying
his prayers, as the train, or cable, drew near the getting-
off station."

Phaeton and I burst out laughing.

"I'm afraid you're only making fun of our invention," said Ned.

"Not I," said Jack. "I like to encourage the inventive faculty in boys."

"Well, then, tell us honestly," said Ned,—"where would you introduce it first? Would you go to New York, and build it under Broadway at once? Or would you go slow, and try it first in this town, on a rather small scale?"

"I think I'd go slow," said Jack.

"And where would be the best place to build it?"

"You'll have to survey the town," said Jack, "and find out where there is the most travel."

"We thought we'd dig the tunnel ourselves," said Ned, "and then give a mortgage on the tunnel, and raise the money to buy the cable."

"I see you have the true business idea," said Jack. "In that case, I think you'd better build it wherever you find the softest dirt."

"That's worth thinking about," said Ned. "And now, Jack, I'll tell you what 'tis. We don't want to throw you out of employment; and when our road's running, and this one stops, you shall have a good situation on ours. There won't be any signal stations, but you may be the train-despatcher—the one that chops off the cable, you know."

"Thank you," said Jack. "I'll think about it."

"It will probably be good pay," said Ned, "and it's certain to be lots of fun."

"Oh, there can be no doubt whatever about that," said Jack, drily.

"Good morning!"

"Good morning!"

"Jack-in-the-Box takes a deep interest in our invention," said Ned, in a low, confidential tone, as we walked away. "I can see that he thinks it's going to be a great success."

Phaeton burst out laughing.

"What are you laughing about?" said Ned.

"I am laughing to think how Jack-in-the-Box fooled you to the top of your bent."

"What do you mean?"

"I mean that the thing won't do at all; and he saw it would n't, as soon as he looked at it; but he thought he would n't say so. He just liked to hear you talk."

"Do you think so?" said Ned to me.

"I'm afraid it's true," said I.

"Well," said Ned, growing a little red in the face, "I don't care. It's no invention of mine, anyway. It was all your idea, Fay."

"Oh, was it?" said Phaeton. "When I heard you talk to Jack-in-the-Box about it, I began to think it was all yours."

"If I was going to make an invention," said Ned, "I'd make one that would work—something practical."

"All right," said Phaeton; "you're at liberty to do so if you wish. I should be glad if you would."

"Well, I will," said Ned. "I'll make one to beat yours all hollow."

Three or four days afterward, Ned came to me with a look on his face that showed he had something important in his mind.

"Can you go?" said he, almost in a whisper.

"That depends on where you're going," said I.

"To see Jack-in-the-Box," said he.

"Yes, I always like to go to the Box," said I. "But I've got to split these kindlings first."

"Oh, never mind your kindlings! You can split those any time. I've got a sure thing now; and if Jack says it's all right, I'll let you go partnership."

Of course, this was more important than any paltry consideration of lighting the fires next morning; so I threw down the hatchet, and we started.

"I think we'd better go by the postern," said I.

Postern was a word we had found frequently used in "The Haunted Castle;" and we had looked out its meaning in the dictionary. Whenever we thought it desirable to get away from the house without being seen,— as, for instance, when we were leaving kindlings unsplit, —we climbed over the back fence, and called it "going by the postern."

3

"All right," said Ned, for in these things he was a wise boy, and a word to him was sufficient.

"What is it?" said I, as soon as we were fairly out of sight of the house. "Tell me all about it."

"Wait till we get to Jack's," said he.

"Has your Aunt Mercy given you money to make a muddle of it?" said I.

"That troubles me a little—that fifteen dollars," said Ned. "You see, we got it honestly; we thought Fay's invention was going to be a great thing, and we must have money to start. But now, if Aunt Mercy knew it was a failure, it would look to her very much as if we had swindled her."

"Not if you gave her back the money," said I.

"But I don't exactly like to do that," said Ned. "It's always a good thing to have a little money. And, besides, she'd lose faith in me, and think I could n't invent anything. And next time, when we had really made a good thing, she'd think it was only another failure, and would n't furnish the money. That's one reason why I made this invention that I have in my pocket now. We can use the money on this, and tell Aunt Mercy we changed off from the Underground Railroad to a better thing."

"How do you do to-day, Jack?"

"Pretty well, thank you! How are you? Come in, boys; I'm glad to see you."

" Would you be willing to look at another invention for us ? "

" Certainly ; with the greatest pleasure."

" I hope it will turn out to be better than the other— that is, more practical," said Ned. " But you see, Jack, that was our first invention, and I suppose we can only improve by practice."

" That is about the only way," said Jack. " What is your second invention ? "

Ned drew a bit of paper from his pocket.

" The other day," said he, " I heard Father reading a piece in the newspaper about a church that was struck by lightning, although it had a lightning-rod. The reason was, that the rod was broken apart at one place, and nobody had noticed it, or if they had, they did n't take the trouble to fix it. People are always careless about those things. And so they lost their church. Father says there are a good many things that spoil lightning-rods. He says, if there's rust in the joints they won't work."

" That's true," said Jack.

" Well, then, all this set me to thinking whether I could n't invent a lightning-rod that would be a sure thing. And here you have it," said Ned, as he unfolded his paper.

Jack looked at it.

" I don't understand it," said he, "you'll have to explain."

"Of course you don't," said Ned. "I will explain."
Jack said he was all attention.

"What does fire do to ice?" said Ned, taking on
the tone of a school-master.

"Melts it," said Jack.

"Right," said Ned. "And when ice is melted, it
becomes what?"

NED'S INVENTION.

"Water," said Jack.

"Right again!" said Ned. "And water does what
to fire?"

"Puts it out," said Jack.

"Exactly so," said Ned. "And there you have it—
action and reaction. That's the principle."

I think Ned borrowed his style of explanation not
so much from the school-master as from a young man

who appeared in the streets one day, selling a sort of stuff to clean the teeth, calling a crowd around him, and trying it on the teeth of one or two boys.

" That's all true," said Jack ; " but how do you apply it to lightning-rods ? "

" Here is a picture," said Ned, " of a house with a rod on it. The family think it's all right, and don't feel afraid when it thunders. But that rod may be broken somewhere, or may be rusted in the joints, and they not know it. What then ? We simply fasten a large ball of ice—marked I in the illustration—to the rod at R—freeze it on tight. You see it is n't likely there will be any break, or any rusty joint, between the point of the rod and the ball."

" Not likely," said Jack.

" But there may be one lower down."

" There may be," said Jack ; " though there could n't be one higher down."

Ned was too intent on his invention to notice this criticism on his expression.

" We'll say a thunder-storm comes up," said he. " The lightning strikes this rod. What then ? In an instant, in the flash of an eye, the lightning melts that ball of ice—it becomes water—in another instant that water puts out the lightning—and the family are safe ! "

" It will if there's enough of it," said Jack.

" Oh, well," said Ned, " if there should happen to be

a little lightning left over, that was n't put out, why, you see, as lightning-rods are *generally* in good order, it would probably be carried off in the usual manner, without doing any harm."

Jack sat with the paper in his hand, and looked at it in silence, as if he were spell-bound.

"What do you think of it?" said Ned.

"I think it's a work of genius," said Jack.

"I'm glad you think so," said Ned.

"And yet," said Jack, "some things that exhibit great genius, don't work well in practice."

"Certainly!" said Ned. "That was the way with Fay's Underground Railroad."

Jack smiled, and nodded.

"And now," continued Ned, "how would you go to work to introduce it? You would n't like to take it and introduce it to the public yourself, would you?—on shares, you know,—you take half of the profits, and we half."

Jack said his business engagements would n't permit him to go into it at present.

"Then we must manage it ourselves. Where would you advise us to put it first?"

"On a tall hickory-tree in Burke's woods," said Jack.

"Why so?" said Ned.

"Because the great trouble's going to be with the lightning that's left over. You don't know what that may do."

"I'm afraid the invention does n't look practical to you," said Ned.

Before Jack could answer, Isaac Holman appeared at the door of the box, with a Latin grammar under his arm. At that time of day, there was an interval of an hour and a half when no train passed, and Isaac had arranged to come and take of Jack a daily lesson in Latin.

"I see it's time for your school to begin; we'll finish talking about this some other day," said Ned, as he hastily thrust the paper into his pocket. For he did n't want Isaac (nor anybody else, I guess) to know about it.

"Don't hurry yourself; I can wait awhile," said Isaac.

"To-morrow will do as well for us," said Ned.

"*Totus dexter!*—all right!" said Isaac, as we left the box, and made room for him to enter.

Isaac had been studying the language only a fortnight, but was fond of using Latin expressions in talking to the boys. Yet he was very considerate about it, and always gave an immediate translation, as in the sentence just quoted.

As Ned and I walked away, I was the first to speak.

"Ned, I have an idea! That ball of ice would only stay on in winter."

"I suppose so," said Ned, a little gloomily.

"And nearly all the thunder-storms are in summer," said I.

"I'm afraid they are," said Ned. "And this invention is n't worth a cent. It's not any better than Fay's." And he tore up the paper, and threw the pieces into the gutter.

"Then what will you do with the fifteen dollars?" said I, after another pause.

"That's a thing we must think about," said he. "But here comes Jimmy the Rhymer. I wonder if he has anything new to-day."

CHAPTER V.

JIMMY THE RHYMER.

JAMES REDMOND, the boys used to say, was small for his
size and old for his age. He was not exactly hump-
backed, but his shoulders came so nearly up to the level
of his ears that he seemed so ; and he was not exactly
an invalid, though we never counted on him in any of
the games or enterprises that required strength or fleet-
ness. I have no idea what his age was. He must have
been some years older than I, and yet all the boys in my
set treated him tenderly and patronizingly, as if he were
a little fellow who needed their encouragement and pro-
tection.

Jimmy used to make little ballads, generally taking for
his subject some incident that had occurred among the
boys of the neighborhood, and often sticking to the facts
of the case—at the expense of rhyme and rhythm—with a
literalness that made him valuable as a historian, whatever he was as a poet. He was called "Jimmy the
Rhymer," and the polite thing to do, on meeting him,
was to ask him if he had anything new to-day—meaning

3*

any new poem.   If he had, he was always willing to read
it, sometimes accompanying it with remarks in prose that
were quite as entertaining as the ballad itself.

" Hello, Jimmy ! "

" Hello, boys ! "

" Got anything new to-day ? "

" Not much."

" That means that you have something."

" Well, yes ; a little one.   But I don't think very
much of it."

This did n't satisfy us.   Jimmy, like many greater artists, was a poor judge of his own productions.   Some of
his ballads of which he had been proudest were so long
and dull that we had almost told him they were failures ;
but it would have required a very hard-hearted boy
to say anything unpleasant to Jimmy.   Others, which
he thought little of, the boys would call for again and
again.

" Let us hear it, please," said Ned.

" I'm afraid I've left it at home," said Jimmy, feeling
in his pockets.   " Oh, no ; here it is."

So we sat down on the horse-block in front of the
Quaker meeting-house, and while Ned whittled the edge
of the block—which had not been rounded off quite
enough, by previous jack-knives, to suit his fancy—
Jimmy read his newest ballad.

" It is called 'The Unlucky Fishermen,'" said he ;

"and you will probably recognize some of the characters.

> " Joe Chase and Isaac Holman,
> They would a-fishing go ;
> They rose at sunrise Friday morn,
> And called their dog Fido."

" What ! " said Ned, interrupting, " the little yellow cur that Joe bought of Clam Jimmy for a six-pence ? "

" Yes, that's the one."

" But his name is n't Fido—it's Prince. Have n't you ever noticed that the smaller and snarlier and more worthless a dog is, the surer it is to be called Prince ? "

" Perhaps that's the way with princes," said Jimmy, who had more than once uttered the most extreme democratic sentiments, expressing contempt for all royalty, merely because it was royalty. " But I don't know,—I never saw one. At any rate, I did n't know the dog's name, and I had to call him something. I think you'll find that everything else is correctly stated."

I ventured to suggest that it did n't make much difference whether the dog's name was right or wrong, in a poem.

" Oh, yes, it does," said Jimmy. " I always try to have my poems true to life ; and I shall change that, and make it Prince—that is, after I have inquired of Joe, and found out that the dog's name really is Prince. I am glad you spoke about it."

Then he continued the reading.

"In two small willow baskets —
    One white, the other brown —
Their mothers put the dinners up
    Which they were to put down.

"They'd dug their bait the night before,—
    The worms were live and thick;
Their bamboo poles were long and strong,
    Their hooks were Limerick."

"My brother Fay says there is n't a Limerick hook in this whole town," said Ned.

"You can buy plenty of them at Karl's—two for a cent," said Jimmy.

"Oh, no, you can't," said Ned. "Fay says you can't get a Limerick hook this side of New York."

"What is a Limerick hook?" said I, for I was not much of a fisherman.

"Why, don't you know?" said Jimmy. "A hook that's made like a little file on the end where you tie the line, instead of a flat knob."

"A real Limerick hook is one that's made in Limerick," said Ned. "Those you get in this town are made in Connecticut, and are only imitations."

I began to suspect that Ned had been nettled at the failure of his lightning-rod invention, and was venting his spite on poor Jimmy's literary invention.

"I can't see," said I, "that it makes any difference

with the poem, whether they were real Limerick hooks, or only imitation. The poetry is just as good."

"Oh, no, it is n't," said Jimmy; "and I'm glad to have my attention called to it. I'll inquire about that, and if I find they were not true Limericks, I'll change that line." Then the reading proceeded.

> "'Now let us make it doubly sure
> That nothing's left,' said Joe.
> And 'Totus dexter!' Ike replied —
> Which means 'All right!' you know.
>
> "These jolly boys set off at once
> When everything was found ;
> Their fathers said, 'We wish good luck!'
> Their mothers, 'Don't get drowned!'"

"Holman's father has n't been at home for four months," said Ned. "He's gone to Missouri to see about an iron mine."

"I admit," said Jimmy, "that there I drew a little on my imagination. I did n't know what they said, and so I put in what I thought they would be likely to say. But if Holman's father was n't at home, of course he could n't have said anything at all. However, I think you'll find that the rest of the poem is entirely true to nature.

> "When they unto the river came,
> Where they should cast the lead,
> The dew still glistened under foot,
> The robin sang o'erhead."

"I doubt if any robin sings so late in the season as this," said Ned.

"Still," said Jimmy, "if one did sing, it would certainly be overhead, and not on the ground. No robin ever sings when he's on the ground. You admit that?"

"Oh, certainly," said Ned.

"Then I think that line may stand as it is," said Jimmy.

> "All down the road and through the woods
>   They had a lovely walk;
> The dog did frisk, and chase the birds,
>   And they did laugh and talk."

"He's been anything but a frisky dog when I've seen him," said Ned.

"Perhaps so," said Jimmy; "but there are exceptions to all rules.

> "But here their luck all left them —
>   The case seemed very sad:
> For everything was good before —
>   Now everything was bad.
>
> "Their sinkers were not large enough,
>   The current was so strong,
> And so they tied on pebble-stones,
>   To help the thing along.
>
> "And bitterly they did regret
>   They bought their lines at Karl's;
> For every time they hauled them out,
>   They found them full of snarls."

"Of course they did," said Ned. "There's not a thing in Karl's store that's not a cheat — all imitation."

"I am glad to hear you say so," said Jimmy. "I thought you would see that the rest of the poem was true to nature.

> "When little fish got on the hooks,
>   They soon flopped off again;
> When big ones bit, they gave a jerk,
>   And snapped the line in twain."

"Isaac told me," said Jimmy, interrupting himself, "that that thing happened every time with him, and every time but once with Joe."

"He probably said that as an excuse for coming home with no fish," said Ned.

"Oh, no,—Ike would n't lie about it," said Jimmy. "He's one of the most truthful boys I ever knew."

"Everybody lies about fishing," said Ned. "It's considered the proper thing to do. That's what they mean by a fish-story."

"But I saw the lines myself," said Jimmy. And then he hurried on with the reading.

> "The dog lay by the dinners,
>   And was told to guard them well —
> To let no stranger, man or beast,
>   Come near, touch, taste, or smell.

" But Fido—of course I mean Prince—fell asleep, and kicked
    The baskets in a dream ;
  The contents tumbled o'er the bank,
    And floated down the stream.

" And once a bass robbed Isaac's hook,
    Just as he tried to haul ;
  Which made him nervous, and in haste
    He let the bait-box fall."

" How could he know what kind of fish it was that
robbed his hook ? " said I.

" I did n't think to ask," said Jimmy.   " But, at any
rate, he said it was a bass, and Isaac is generally pretty
correct.

" It fell between two rugged rocks,
    Where out of reach it lay ;
  And when with sticks they fished it up,
    The worms had crawled away.

" Now when the golden setting sun
    Was shining down the glen,
  They sadly turned their steps toward home,
    These luckless fishermen.

" And when they came upon the road,
    All tired in foot and side,
  They said, ' Let's hide our poles away,
    And try to catch a ride.'

" They caught upon an omnibus —
    They did not stir or talk ;
  But some one cried out, ' Whip behind ! '
    And so they had to walk."

"That must have been a Dublin boy," said Ned. "Nobody on our side of the river is mean enough to holler ' whip behind !' "

"I think it was a Dublin boy," said Jimmy. "If I can find out for certain, I shall state it so in the poem.

> "They came up slowly from the gate,
>   And Fido—that is to say, Prince—walked behind ;
> Their parents sat about the door,
>   Or on the grass reclined.
>
> "Their fathers said—at least Joe's father did—' It grieves us much
>   That you no luck have found.'
> Their mothers said, 'Our precious boys,
>   We're glad you are not drowned.' "

"That's a good poem," said I, as we rose from the horse-block. "I like that."

"Yes," said Ned; "it ought to be printed."

"I'm glad to hear you say so," said Jimmy. "But I think I can improve it in a few spots, if I can get at the facts. At any rate, I shall try."

Jimmy continued his walk up the street, while we sauntered toward home.

"I think you were too severe in your criticisms on the poem," said I. "I'm afraid Jimmy felt hurt."

"Do you think so?" said Ned. "Well, now, I did n't mean to be. I would n't hurt that boy's feelings for the world. I suppose I must have been a little cross on account of my lightning-rod. But I should n't have played it off on Jimmy, that's a fact."

" I think he has great genius," said I, " and it ought to be encouraged."

" Yes, it ought," said Ned. " I've often thought so, myself, and wished I could do something for him. Perhaps I can, now that I have capital. Father says nothing can be done without capital."

" Jimmy's folks are very poor," said I.

" That's so," said Ned. " I don't suppose his father ever had fifteen dollars at one time in his life. Do you think of any good way in which I could help him with a little capital ? "

" I don't know of any way, unless it is to print his poems. I should think if his poems could once be published, he might make a great deal of money out of them, and be able to support himself, and perhaps help his mother a little."

" That's so," said Ned. " I'll publish his poems for him. Come over after supper, and we'll talk it up."

CHAPTER VI.

THE PRICE OF POETRY.

WHEN I went over in the evening, I found that Ned had gone to Jimmy's house, and obtained thirteen of his poems in manuscript, and was now carefully looking them over, correcting what he considered errors.

"I tell you what 'tis," said he, "Jimmy's an awful good poet, but he needs somebody to look out for his facts."

"Do you find many mistakes?" said I.

"Yes; quite a few. Here, for instance, he calls it a mile from the Four Corners to Lyell street. I went with the surveyors when they measured it last summer, and it was just seven eighths of a mile and three rods over."

"But you could n't very well say 'seven eighths of a mile and three rods over' in poetry," said I.

"Perhaps not," said Ned; "and yet it wont do to have that line stand as it is. It 'll be severely criticised by everybody who knows the exact distance."

I felt that Ned was wrong, but I could not tell how or why. In later years I have learned that older people than he confidently criticise what they don't understand,

and put their own mechanical patches upon the artistic work of others.

"Perhaps we'd better see what Fay thinks about it," said I. "He probably knows more about poetry than we do."

"He's in the library, getting Father to help him on a hard sum," said Ned. "He'll be here in a minute."

When Phaeton returned, we pointed out the difficulty to him.

"That's all right," said he. "That's poetic license."

"What is poetic license?" said I.

"Poetic license," said Phaeton, "is a way that poets have of making things fit when they don't quite fit."

"Like what?" said Ned.

"Like this," said Phaeton; "this is as good an example as any. You see, he could n't say 'seven eighths of a mile and three rods over,' because that would be too long."

"That would be the exact distance," said Ned.

"I mean it would make this line too long," said Phaeton; "and, besides, it has to rhyme with that other line, which ends with the word *style*."

"And if that other line ended with *cheek*, would he have to call it a *league* from the Four Corners to Lyell street?" said Ned.

"I suppose so," said Phaeton, "though it would n't be a very good rhyme."

" And is that considered all right ? "

" I believe it is."

" Then you can't depend upon a single statement in any poem." said Ned.

" Oh, yes, you can," said Phaeton—" a great many."

" Mention one," said Ned.

> " ' Thirty days hath September,
> April, June, and November,' "

said Phaeton.

" That's true," said Ned ; " but it's only because the words happen to come so. At any rate, you've greatly lessened my respect for poetry, and I don't know whether I'd better publish them, after all."

" These poems ?—were you going to publish them ? " said Phaeton.

" Yes."

" Why ? "

" To make a little money for Jimmy. You know his folks are very poor," said Ned.

" The papers wont pay you anything for them," said Phaeton. " Alec Barnes's sister had a poem two columns long in the *Vindicator* last week, and Alec told me she did n't get a cent for it."

" But we're going to make a book of them," said Ned. " You can make money on a book, can't you ? "

" I believe you can," said Phaeton. " Wait a minute."

He went to the library, and came back with three volumes of a cyclopædia, out of which, after looking through several articles, he got, at intervals, these bits of information :

" Moore received three thousand guineas for ' Lalla Rookh.' "

" How much is that ? " said Ned.

" Over fifteen thousand dollars," said Phaeton.

" Whew ! " said Ned.

" Scott made a profit of ten thousand dollars on ' The Lady of the Lake.' "

" Good gracious ! " said Ned.

" Byron received more than seventy-five thousand dollars for his poems."

" Great Cæsar ! " said Ned.

" Tupper must have made thirty thousand dollars on his ' Proverbial Philosophy.' "

" That's enough ! " said Ned. " That's plenty ! I begin to have great respect for poetry, in spite of the license. And I suppose that if the poets make all that money, the publishers make a little something, too."

" They probably know how to look out for themselves," said Phaeton. " But who is going to publish this book for you ? "

" I'm going to publish it myself. You know we have n't used up the capital I got from Aunt Mercy," said Ned.

" But you're not a publisher."

" Nobody is a publisher until after he has published something," said Ned.

" But that won't be capital enough to print a book," said Phaeton. " Printing costs like fury."

" Then I shall have to get more from Aunt Mercy."

" Yes, I suppose you can—she'd give you anything ; but, the truth is, Ned, I—I had a little plan of my own about that."

" About what ? "

" About the fifteen dollars—or a part of it. I don't think I should need all of it."

" What is it ? Another foolish invention ? "

" Yes, it is a sort of invention ; but it is sure to go—sure to go."

" Let's hear all about it," said Ned.

" Will you lend me the money to try it ? "

" How much will it take ? "

" Six or eight dollars, I should think."

" Yes ; I'll lend you six dollars on it. Or, if it is really a good thing, I'll put in the six dollars as my share, and go partnership."

" Well, then, it's a substitute for a balloon," said Phaeton. " Much cheaper, and safer, and better in every way."

" How does it work ? " said Ned.

" It makes a horizontal ascension. I could tell you

all about it; but I would rather wait a week, and then show you."

" All right!" said Ned. " You can have the money, and we'll wait."

" Thank you!" said Phaeton. " But now tell me how you are going to publish Jimmy's poems."

" Why, just publish them, of course," said Ned.

" And what do you understand by that?"

" Take this copy to the printer, and tell him to print the books. When it's done, load them into big wagons, and drive around to the four book-stores and leave them. After a few days, call around and get the money, and divide with Jimmy. We would n't ask them to pay for them till they had a chance to look them over, and see how they liked them."

" I don't believe that would work," said Phaeton.

" Why not?" said Ned.

" The booksellers might not take them."

" Not take them!" said Ned. " They'd be only too glad to. Of course they would make a profit on them. I suppose the price would be—well, about half a dollar; and we should let them have them for—well, say for forty-seven cents apiece. Maybe if they took a large number, and paid cash down, they might have them for forty-five."

Phaeton laughed.

" They don't do business for any such small profits as that," said he.

"I've heard Father tell of a man," said Ned, "that made his fortune when wheat rose three cents on a bushel. And who would n't rather have a volume of Jimmy's poems than a bushel of wheat? If nobody happened to buy the wheat for a year or two, it would spoil; but that volume of poems could stand on the shelf in the book-store for twenty years, and be just as good at the end of that time as the day it was put there."

"All that sounds very well," said Phaeton; "but you'd better talk with some one that knows about it, before you rush into the enterprise."

"I'll go and see Jack-in-the-Box, of course," said Ned. "He must know all about books. I never yet asked him anything that he did n't know all about."

Ned could hardly wait for the night to pass away, and when the next day came, off we posted once more to see Jack-in-the-Box. When we got there, Ned plunged at once into the business, before we had fairly said good morning.

"Jack," said he, "did you ever publish a book?"

Jack blushed, and asked why he wanted to know.

"I am thinking of publishing one," said Ned.

"Indeed?" said Jack. "I did n't know that you had written one."

"I have n't," said Ned. "Jimmy the Rhymer wrote it. But I talk of publishing it."

"I see," said Jack. "I did n't understand you before."

4

"I thought you would understand all about it," said Ned.

"Your expression might have meant either one of two things," said Jack. "When a publisher prints a book and sells it, he of course is said to publish it; and when a person writes a book, and gets a publisher to publish it for him, he also is said to have published a book."

"I see," said Ned. "And did you ever publish one?"

"I never was a publisher," said Jack.

"Still, you may know a good deal about it."

"I know a little about it," said Jack, "and shall be glad to give you all the advice I can. Is this the manuscript?"

Ned said it was, and handed him a roll which he had brought in his hand.

"Ah, poetry, I see," said Jack, turning over the leaves.

"Yes, first-rate poetry," said Ned. "A few licenses here and there; but that can't be helped, you know."

"Of course not," said Jack.

"We want to make as much money as we can," said Ned, "for Jimmy's folks are awful poor, and he needs it, and poetry's the stuff to make money."

"Is it?" said Jack. "I'm glad to hear it."

"There was Sir Walter Tupper," said Ned, "made

thirty thousand dollars, clean cash, on a poem called 'The Lady and the Snake'—probably not half so good as these of Jimmy's. Who'd want to read about such a dreadful thing? And Mr. Barrons was paid seventy-five thousand dollars for his poem called 'The Little Rook,' whatever that is. And there was Lord Moore got three thousand guineas—that's fifteen thousand dollars, you know—for some sort of philosophy all turned into rhyme. I don't see how a philosophy could be in rhyme, though, for you know everything in philosophy has to be exact, and in poetry you have to take licenses. Suppose you came to the five mechanical powers, and the line before ended with *sticks*, what could you do? You'd have to say there were *six* of them."

Jack laughed heartily.

"Yes, it would be ridiculous," continued Ned. "But that's Lord Moore's lookout. In these poems of Jimmy's, there is n't any trouble of that sort. They don't need to be exact. Suppose, for instance, one of them says it's a mile from the Four Corners to Lyell street. What odds? Very few people know that it's just seven eighths of a mile and three rods over. I might not have known it myself, if I had n't happened to be with the surveyors when they measured it. Jimmy admits that he has drawn on his imagination in one or two places; but he is n't going to do it any more, and I think those can be fixed up somehow."

Jack laughed again, said he thought imagination was not altogether objectionable in poetry, and kept on turning over the leaves.

" Where is the title-page ? " said he.

" What is that ? " said Ned.

" The one with the name on it—the first page in the book," said Jack.

" Oh ! " said Ned, " we never thought about that. Wont the printer make it himself ? "

" Not unless you write it first."

" Then we've got to name the book before we go any further," said Ned.

" That's it, exactly," said Jack.

" Could n't you name it for us ? "

" I might suggest some names," said Jack, " and let you choose ; but it seems to me, the person who wrote it ought to name it."

" Oh, never mind Jimmy," said Ned.   " He'll be satisfied with anything I do."

" It might be called simply, ' Poems. By Jimmy the Rhymer,' " said Jack.

" His name is James Redmond," said Ned.

" I'll write down a few," said Jack, as he reached into the box under his chair and took out a sheet of paper and a pencil, and in five minutes he showed us the list :

" Rhymes and Roundelays. By James Redmond."

" A Picnic on Parnassus. By James Redmond."

" The Unlucky Fishermen, and other Poems. By James Redmond."

" Jimmy's Jingles."

" Songs of a School-boy."

" Minutes with the Muses. By James Redmond."

It did not take Ned very long to choose the third of these titles, which he thought " sounded the most sensible."

" Very well," said Jack, as he wrote a neat title-page and added it to the manuscript. " And how are you going to publish it ? "

" I thought I'd get you to tell me how," said Ned, who by this time had begun to suspect that he knew very little about it.

" The regular way," said Jack, " would be to send it to a firm in New York, or Boston, or Philadelphia."

" And then what ? "

" They would have a critic read it and tell them whether it was suitable."

" He'd be sure to say it was ; but then what ? "

" Then they would have it printed and bound, and advertise it in the papers, and sell it, and send it to other stores to be sold."

" But where would our profits come from ? "

" Oh, they would pay you ten per cent. on all they sold."

" And how many do you think they would sell ? "

" Nobody can tell," said Jack.   " Different books sell differently—all the way from none at all up to a great many."

Ned borrowed Jack's pencil, and figured for two or three minutes.

" Then," said he, " if they should sell a hundred of our book, we would only get five dollars—two and a half for Jimmy, and two and a half for me."

" That's about it," said Jack.

" Then that won't do," said Ned.   " Jimmy's folks are very poor, and he needs more than that.   Is n't there some way to make more money out of it ? "

" Not unless you pay for the printing and binding yourself," said Jack.

" And how much would that cost ? "

Jack looked it over and said he guessed about two hundred dollars for an edition of five hundred.

" We can't do it," said Ned, with a sigh.   " Aunt Mercy would n't give me so much money at a time."

" There is one other way," said Jack.

" How is it ? "

" To get up a little printing-office of your own, and print it yourselves."

" That sounds like business ; I guess you've hit it," said Ned, brightening up.   " How much money would it take for that ? "

"I should think twenty-five or thirty dollars would get up a good one."

"Then we can do it," said Ned. "Aunt Mercy will let me have that, right away."

"Do you know anything about printing?" said Jack.

"Not much; but my brother Fay knows all about it. He worked in a printing-office one vacation, to earn money to buy him a chest of tools."

"Indeed! what did your brother do in the printing-office?" said Jack.

"They called him second devil," said Ned, "but he was really a roller-boy."

"They're the same thing," said Jack. "There's no harm in a printer's devil; he's only called so because he sometimes gets pretty well blacked up with the ink."

"I'm glad to hear you say so," said Ned, who had been a little ashamed to tell what Fay did in the office, but now began to think it might be rather honorable. "In fact, he was first devil one week, when the regular first devil was gone to his grandfather's funeral in Troy."

"Then he knows something about the business," said Jack; "and perhaps I can help you a little. I understand the trade to some extent."

"Of course you do," said Ned. "You understand everything. And after we've finished Jimmy's book, we can print all sorts of other things—do a general business, in fact. I'll see what Fay says, and if he'll go in, we'll start it at once."

While Ned was uttering the last sentence, Jack's alarm-clock went off, and Jack took his flag and went out to flag the Pacific express, while we walked away. We must have been very much absorbed in the new project, for we never even turned to look at the train ; and a train of cars in swift motion is a sight that few people can help stopping to look at, however busy they may be.

Readers who have followed this story thus far will perhaps inquire where the scene of it is laid. I think it is a pertinent question, yet there is a sort of unwritten law among story-writers against answering it, excepting in some vague, indefinite way; and I have transgressed so many written laws, that I should like at least to keep the unwritten ones. But if you are good at playing "buried cities," I will give you a chance to find out the name of that inland city where Phaeton and his companions dwelt. I discovered it buried, quite unintentionally, in one of Jimmy the Rhymer's poems. Here is the couplet:

"Though his head to the north wind so often is bared,
At the sound of the siroc he's terribly scared."

CHAPTER VII.

PHAETON'S CHARIOT.

NED and I pushed on the project for a printing-office with great energy. We made the acquaintance of a man named Alvord, who kept a job office—where they never seemed to be in a hurry, as they always were in the newspaper offices—and was never unwilling to answer questions or sell us old type. It was great fun to explore the mysteries of his establishment. I think he liked boys as much as Jack-in-the-Box did, and I'm sure it was a pleasure to us, in laying out Ned's capital, to pay so much of it to so pleasant a man.

But energy without skill is like zeal without knowledge ; in fact, it is about the same thing, and we could n't really make much progress till Phaeton should take hold ; and he would have nothing to do with it till he had finished his apparatus for "a horizontal balloon-ascension," which he was at work upon every minute that he could spare from sleep and meals.

With the help of the carriage-maker and the blacksmith, and Ned's capital—which he drew upon much more freely than had been bargained for—he constructed

4*

a low, broad, skeleton-like carriage, the body of which was hung below the axles of the wheels, instead of above them, and almost touched the ground. This was to prevent it from tipping over easily. The front axle turned on a swivel, and was controlled by two stout handles, by means of which the carriage could be steered. On the front of the box were three iron hooks. At the back there was a single hook. The wheels were pretty large, but the whole was made as light as possible.

When it was finished, Phaeton brought it home and put it away carefully in the wood-shed.

" I am afraid," said he, " that somebody will steal this car, or come in and damage it, unless we put a lock on this wood-shed door."

" Who would want to steal it or damage it ? " said Ned.

" The Dublin boys," said Phaeton, half under his breath. " Two of them were seen prowling around here the other day."

One section of the town, which was divided from ours by the deep gorge of the river, was popularly known as Dublin, and the boys who lived there, though probably very much like other boys, were always considered by us as our natural enemies—plotters against the peace of boy society, capable of the most treacherous designs and the darkest deeds ever perpetrated in the juvenile world. Every piece of mischief not obviously to be accounted for in any other way, was laid to the Dublin boys as a matter of course.

"But we have n't any padlock," said Ned, "except that old brass one, and the key of that is lost, and we could n't turn it when we had it."

"I suppose we shall have to buy a new one," said Phaeton.

"All right—buy one," said Ned.

"I have n't any money," said Phaeton.

"Nor I," said Ned—"spent the last cent for a beautiful little font of Tuscan type; weighed just five pounds, fifteen cents a pound—nothing the matter with it, only the Es are gone."

"The Es are gone?" said Phaeton. "Do you mean to say that you have been buying a font of type with no Es in it?"

"Yes; why? What's the harm in that?" said Ned. "You don't expect everything to be perfect when you buy things second-hand."

"Of course not," said Phaeton; "but what can you do without Es? If the Qs or the Xs were gone, it would n't so much matter; but there's hardly a word that has n't at least one E in it. Just count the Es on a page of any book. And you've been fooling away your money on a font of type with no Es! Mr. Alvord ought to be ashamed of himself to cheat a boy like that."

"You need n't be scolding me for fooling away the

money," said Ned. " What have you been doing, I should like to know ? Fooling away the money on that old torrid-zontal balloon thing, which will probably make a shipwreck of you the first time you try it. And, besides, I did n't buy the type of Mr. Alvord."

" Where did you get it ? " ·

" Bought it of a boy that I met on the stairs when I was coming down from Alvord's."

" Who was he ? "

" I don't know. He lives on one of those cross-streets down by the aqueduct. I went to his house with him to get the type. He said he used to have a little office, but his father would n't let him keep it any more, just because the baby ate some of the ink."

" It's too bad," said Phaeton ; " the type will never be of any use. What do you suppose could have become of the Es ? "

" I don't know," said Ned, a little morosely, " unless the baby sister ate them too."

" They'd set rather heavy on her stomach," said Phaeton. " But how are we going to get a lock for this door ? "

" I don't see that we can get one at all," said Ned.

I suggested that the door of the wood-shed might be nailed up, to keep out the Dublin boys, till we had a chance to get a padlock.

" That's a first-rate idea," said Phaeton, and he at

once brought out the hammer and nail-box, and began to nail up the door. It was a heavy, panelled door, which had evidently come from some old mansion that was torn down.

"It's as well to make it strong while we're about it," said he; "for if those fellows should come, they'd pry it open if they could," and he put in a few more nails.

"Father showed me how to drive nails so as to make them hold," said I. "Let me show you;" and taking the hammer from his hand, I drove eight or ten more nails into the door, driving them in pairs, each pair slanting in opposite directions.

"That's a thing worth knowing," said Ned. "Let me practice on it a little."

He took the hammer, and drove one or two pairs in the manner I had shown him, and was so pleased with his success, that he kept on till he had used up all the nails in the box.

"No Dublin boy is going to get that car this night," said he, as he gave a final blow to the last nail.

"No," said Phaeton; "I think that's pretty safe."

As it began to rain, I was obliged to hurry home. That night, as I afterward learned, there was sorrow in the breast of the youngest member of the Rogers family. Little May Rogers, who never went to sleep without her favorite cat, Jemima, curled up on the foot of her little bed, could n't go to sleep because Jemima was nowhere to be found in the house, and had not come when every out-side door in turn was opened, and she was called from the vasty darkness. Even when Mrs. Rogers stood in the kitchen-door and rasped the carving-knife on the steel, Jemima failed to come bounding in. That was considered decisive as to her fate. The cat would be sure to come at that sound, if she were able to come at all.

But a much more serious commotion shook the family next morning. When Mr. Rogers went down to his breakfast, it was not ready; in fact, the kitchen fire was not made.

" How is this, Biddy ? " said he to the cook.

" Sure, I could n't help it, sir; I could get no kindlings."

" Why so, Biddy ? "

" Because, sir, the wood-shed door's bewitched. I could n't get it open. And everything outside is soakin' wet wid the rain, and so of course I could n't kindle the fire."

Mr. Rogers walked out to the wood-shed door, and attempted to open it with an impatient and vigorous jerk, but the handle came off in his hand. Then he tried to get hold of it by the edge, but there was n't a crack where he could insert his fingers. Then he took hold of it at the bottom, where there was considerable space, but it would not budge a hair. He was becoming a little excited, for he had an engagement to leave town by the early train. He went into the house for some sort of tool, and brought out the poker. Cutting a little hole with his pocket-knife at the edge of the door, he inserted the poker, and pried; but the poker bent double, and the door did not stir. Then he went in again, and brought out the stove-wrench. Cutting the hole a little larger, he pried at the door with the wrench; but the wrench was of cast-iron, and snapped in two.

"Biddy," said he, "I see a light at Robbins's,"—it was very early in the morning—"go over and borrow an axe."

Biddy soon returned with an axe, and Mr. Rogers tried to pry the door open with that, but only succeeded in breaking splinters from the edge.

"Biddy," said he, "bring a light, and let's see what ails it."

Biddy brought out a candle, but trembled so at the idea of letting out the witches, that she dropped it at Mr. Rogers's feet, and it struck on its lighted end and immediately went out.

Biddy made rapid apologies, and ran in for another candle. But Mr. Rogers would wait no longer. He raised the axe in fury, and began to slaughter the door, like a mediæval soldier before the gate of a besieged castle.

Slice after slice was torn off and flew inward, striking the opposite side of the shed; but the door as a whole would not fall. When a considerable hole had been made, a frightened cat, its eyes gleaming wildly, and its tail as large as a feather-duster, leaped out from the inner darkness, passing over Mr. Rogers's head, and knocking his hat off, landed somewhere in the yard, and immediately made for the woods. Biddy, who arrived on the ground with the second candle just in time to witness this performance, dropped the light again, and fled screaming into the house.

This aroused two neighbors, who threw up their windows, thrust their heads out, and, hearing the powerful blows of the axe, thought a maniac was abroad, and hallooed for the police.

The watchman on that beat, ever on the alert, waited only eight or nine minutes, till he could call four others to his aid, when all five of them started for the scene of the trouble. Separating after they had entered Mr. Rogers's gate, they made a little circuit through the yard, and cautiously approached him, two on each side, and one behind. As the one behind laid his hand on his shoulder, Mr. Rogers dropped the axe, whirled around, and "hauled off," as the boys say, but caught the gleam of the silver star on the policeman's breast, and dropped his fist.

"What do you want?" said he.

"If it's you, we don't want anything," said the policeman, who, of course, knew Mr. Rogers very well. "But we thought we wanted a crazy man."

"Then you might as well take me," said Mr. Rogers, "for I am pretty nearly crazy. The mischief has got into this door, so that it could n't be opened, and the cook had no kindlings and I no breakfast; and I shall lose the early train, and if I don't reach Albany to-day, I can't tell how many dollars it will cost me, but a good many."

Mr. Rogers drew out his handkerchief, and wiped the perspiration from his brow.

One of the policemen produced a bull's-eye lantern, and examined the ruined door, passing it up and down the edge where the outer frame, studded with many nails, still clung tightly to the jambs, all the central portion having been cut away in ragged slices.

"This door has been nailed up with a great many nails," said he.

"I can't imagine who would do that," said Mr. Rogers; "this is n't the first day of April."

Neither could the policemen. In fact, I have observed that policemen have very little imagination. In this instance, five of them, all imagining at once, could not imagine who nailed up that door. The nearest they could come to it was, that it was probably done with a heavy, blunt instrument, in the hands of some person or persons unknown.

When, later in the day, we boys stood contemplating what Ned called the "shipwreck of the door"—older people than he call all sorts of wrecks shipwrecks—he re-

marked that he did n't know what his father would say, if
he should find out who did it.

Mr. Rogers had taken the next train for Albany.

" He will find out," said Phaeton ; " for I shall tell
him as soon as he gets home."

The day that his father returned, Phaeton told, at the
tea-table, the whole story of how the door was bewitched. A week had then passed, and—such are the
soothing influences of time—Mr. Rogers laughed heartily
at the whole affair, and at his own excitement most of all.

" I had no idea," said Ned, solemnly, " that so much
trouble could be caused by a few nails."

His mother thought " few " was good.

The next day I heard little May Rogers telling
another child about it. This was her story :

" You see, brother Fay and brother Neddie, they
drived a nail in the wood-shed door; and Biddy, she
lended Mr. Robbins's axe ; and then Papa, he got be-
sited ; and so we haven't any wood-shed door any more."

Meanwhile, the preparations for the horizontal balloon ascension had gone on. But, as Ned remarked
long ago, nothing could be done without capital, and he
was obliged to make another business call upon his Aunt
Mercy.

" What's new down at your house ? " said she, after
the greetings were over.

"Nothing particular," said Ned.

"I hear that idiotic brother of yours has been cutting up a pretty caper," said Aunt Mercy, after a pause.

"What was it?" said Ned.

"Why, don't you know?"

"I don't know what you have been told, and I can't think of anything very bad that Fay has done."

"Gracious me!" said Aunt Mercy. "Don't you call it bad to go around slyly in the night and nail up every door and window in the house?"

"Yes, that would be pretty bad, Aunty. But Fay has n't done so."

"You admit that it was bad, then?"

"Why, certainly—but it is n't true. Only one door was nailed up—the wood-shed door."

"I do believe you're standing up for him. But I tell you, a boy that would nail up one door would nail up a hundred."

"He might if he had nails enough," said Ned, in a low voice.

"That's just it," said Aunt Mercy. "That fellow would nail up just as many doors as he could get nails for. I've no doubt it was only the givin' out of the nails that prevented him from going through every house in the neighborhood. Mark my words, he'll come to some bad end. Don't you have anything to do with him, Edmund Burton."

Ned said he thought it would be rather hard not to have anything to do with his own brother.

"Yes, I suppose so," said Aunt Mercy. "But do the best you can."

"Yes, Aunty, I'll do my best."

"Now tell me," said she, "about your muddle. Have you made a muddle yet?"

I thought Ned might have answered conscientiously that he had made a muddle. But he said:

"No, Aunty, we've put that off for a while. We think it will be best to do some other things first."

"What are the other things?"

"One of them is a printing-office. We think of setting up a little printing-office to print little books and papers and cards and things, if we can get together enough money for it. It takes rather more capital than we have at present."

I suppose Aunt Mercy thought I was the other one besides himself included in Ned's "we."

"I should have supposed," said she, "that it was best to finish one muddle before going into another. But you know best, Edmund Burton. I have great confidence in your judgment." And she leaned back in her chair and closed her eyes, and seemed to be dreaming for some minutes. I doubt if she more than half knew which Edmund Burton she was talking to—the one who had long since gone down beneath the waters of a distant sea, or

the young scapegrace who, without intending to represent anything falsely, had got so much money from her
on false representations.

" I don't know how it is," said he to me one day. " I
never intend to cheat Aunt Mercy ; and yet, whenever
I go to see her, things seem to fix themselves somehow so
that she misunderstands. I guess it's her imagination."

" How much money do you need for your new muddle ? " said she, when she came out of her reverie.

" Jack-in-the-Box says he thinks twenty-five or thirty
dollars would fit up a good one," said Ned.

" Who is Jack-in-the-Box ? "

" A gentleman connected with the railroad."

" Queer name for a railroad director," said Aunt
Mercy. " But I suppose you've blundered on it.
French, very likely. Might be Jacquin Thibaux. (I
studied French two terms at Madam Farron's.) Some
of those old Huguenot names have got into strange
shapes. But it does n't matter. I dare say Monsieur
Thibaux is right about it. I haven't any money with me
to-night, but I'll send it over to you to-morrow. Don't
let that ignorant brother of yours meddle with your
printing-office ; he'll misspell every word, and disgrace
the family."

" I'll try to keep him straight," said Ned. " Good-
night, Aunty."

" Good-night, Edmund Burton, my dear boy."

"I thought part of this capital," said I to Ned, as we walked away, "was for the horizontal balloon."

"So it is," said he; "but I could n't explain that to Aunt Mercy, because Fay has never explained it to me. I have no idea how he's going to make that queer thing go."

When Phaeton was furnished with a little more money, we soon saw how the thing was to go. He built three enormous kites, six feet high. They were not bow-kites—the traditional kite always represented in pictures, but seldom used in our country. They were the far more powerful six-cornered kite, familiar to the boys of the Middle States. He certainly built them with great skill, and Ned and I had the pleasure of helping him—if holding the paste-cup and hunting for material to make the tails was helping.

As each was finished, Phaeton carefully stood it up in the wood-shed to dry, where there was no more danger of Dublin boys; for Mr. Rogers had sent a carpenter to put on a new door and furnish it with a lock. Nevertheless, Phaeton took the first kite to his room for the night, and put it against the wall behind the bed. But Ned, who tossed a great deal, managed to kick a hole through it in his sleep. After that, they were left in the wood-shed over night, where a similar misfortune befell the second. Biddy, breaking kindlings in an unscientific way with the hatchet, sent a piece of wood flying through the kite, tearing a large hole on what a sailor would call the starboard quarter.

When Phaeton complained of her carelessness, she seemed to think she had improved the kite, saying: " The two kites were not comrades before—but they are now."

When an enterprising boy attempts to carry out some little project of his own, it is astonishing to see how even the best natured household will seem to conspire against him. If he happens to leave a few of his things on the dining-room floor, they are carelessly stepped upon by his own mother, or swept out-of-doors by an ignorant servant. I have seen a boy trying to make a galvanic battery, and his sister looking on and fervently hoping it would fail, so that she could have the glass cups to put into her play-house.

However, Phaeton had about as little of this sort of thing to endure as any boy ever had. When the kites were finished and dry, and the holes patched up, and the tails hung, Phaeton said he was ready to harness up his team as soon as the wind was right.

" Which way do you want it ? " said I.

" It must be a steady breeze, straight down the turnpike," said he.

One reason why Phaeton chose this road was, that here he would encounter no telegraph wires. At the railway crossing, two men, riding on loads of hay, had come in contact with the wires and been seriously hurt. Another repetition of the accident might have been prevented by raising the wires on higher poles, but the company had chosen rather to run them down the pole on one side, under the street, and up the next pole.

"But I don't see how these kites are going to work," said Ned, "if you fly them side by side, and hitch the strings to those three hooks."

"Why not?"

"Because they'll interfere with each other, and get all tangled up."

"You would think so," said Phaeton, "if you have n't made a study of kite-flying, as I have. If you look at a dozen boys flying their kites at once on the common, you will see that, no matter how near together two or three boys stand, their kites will not go in exactly the same direction. Either the strings will slant away from each other a little, or else they will cross."

"How do you account for that?" said Ned.

"I suppose it's because you never can make two kites exactly alike; or, if they are exactly alike, they are not hung precisely the same; and so the wind bears a little more on the left side of one, and a little more on the right side of the other."

"I guess that's so," said Ned. "And yet it seems to me it would be better to fly them tandem."

"How would you get them up?" said I.

"First get up one," said Ned. "And when it was well up, fasten the end of the string to the back of the next kite, and let that up, and do the same with the third. Then you would have a straight pull by the whole team in line."

"And the pull of all three kites would come on the last string, and probably break it," said Phaeton.

"I did n't think of that," said Ned. "I see your way is the best, after all. But hurry up and have it over with, for we want you to help us about the printing-office ; we can't get along without you."

"It never will be 'over with,'" said Phaeton. "I shall ride out every fine day, when the wind is in the right direction."

"Why, is that all it's for?" said Ned—"merely your own amusement?"

"Not at all," said Phaeton. "It is a great invention, to be introduced all over the country. Better than a locomotive, because it will run on a common road. Better than horses, because it does n't eat anything. But then, I'm going to enjoy it myself as much as I can. However, we'll find time for the printing."

5

CHAPTER VIII.

A HORIZONTAL BALLOON-ASCENSION.

PHAETON had to wait three days for a fair wind, and in that time the secret—for we had tried to keep it quiet—leaked out among the boys.

It was Saturday, and everything seemed favorable. As Ned and I wanted to go up town in the forenoon, and Phaeton could not start the thing alone, he appointed two o'clock in the afternoon as the hour for the experiment.

On our way up town we met Isaac Holman.

" I'm going down to see your brother's new flying machine, or whatever it is," said he.

" 'T is n't going to start till two o'clock," said Ned.

" *Totus dexter !*—all right! I'll be around at that hour," said Holman.

Phaeton gave his apparatus a thorough inspection, newly greased the wheels, tested every string about the kites, and made sure that all was in perfect order.

Exactly at two o'clock, he took a strong stake and a heavy mallet, walked out into the street, and, amid a babel of questions from about twenty boys, who had grad-ually gathered there, drove the stake exactly in the mid

dle of the road, leaving it a foot and a half out of the
ground. He answered none of the questions, and, in fact,
did not open his lips, except to return the greeting of Holman, who sat on the bowlder by the horse-gate, and was
the only one that asked nothing.

I saw Monkey Roe hanging on the outskirts of the
crowd. His name was James Montalembert Roe ; but
he was never called anything but Monkey Roe, and he
seemed to like it just as well. The moment I saw him, I
began to fear mischief. He was a thoroughly good-natured fellow, but was always plotting some new sort of
fun, and was as full of invention, though in a very different way, as Phaeton himself.

When Phaeton had returned and put away his mallet,
we all took hold of the car and ran it out into the street,
where Phaeton fastened a short rope to the hook at the
back, and tied the other end firmly to the stake.

Then I stood by the car, as a sort of guard, while he
and Ned brought out the kites, one at a time, and got
them up. When each had risen to the full height of the
string, which was pretty long,—and they were the best-
behaved kites I ever saw,—Phaeton tied the string to one
of the hooks on the front of the car.

When all three were harnessed up, they lifted the fore-
wheels from the ground.

This work used up considerable time, and while it was
going on, the crowd about us was increasing by the addi-

tion of Dublin boys, who kept coming, singly or in twos
and threes, and were distinguishable by the fact that they
were all barefooted, without jackets, and had their trousers supported by one suspender buckled around the waist
like a belt.

It seemed evident that somebody had told them about
the horizontal balloon-ascension, for they did not come as
if by accident, but as if by appointment, and made
straight for the car, which they inspected with a great
deal of curiosity.

Phaeton brought out four shot-bags filled with sand,
and placed them in a row in the front of the car.

Then he brought out a rope five or six yards long,
with a small balloon-anchor fastened to it. A balloon-
anchor is made of three iron hooks placed back to back,
so that the points project in three different directions, and
the three backs or shanks welded together into one stem,
which ends in a ring, through which the rope is tied.

Phaeton tied the end of the anchor-rope to the hook
on the back end of his car, coiled it up in one corner of
the box, and laid the anchor on the coil. His calculation
was, that when he threw it out on the road it would
catch a little here and there in the ground, as the hooks
dragged over the surface, making the car go more slowly,
till after a while it would take a firm hold of something
and bring him to a full stop.

Phaeton also brought out a small American flag, on a

light staff, and stuck it up in a place made for it, on one of the back corners of the car.

The kites were now tugging away at the car, with a steady and strong pull. The arrangement was, that when Phaeton was seated (on a light board laid across the top of the car) with the steering handles in his grasp, and all was ready, he would give the word, and I was to draw a sharp knife across the rope that held the car to the stake.

All now was ready. Ned, who had gone down the road a short distance, to see if any teams were coming, signalled that the coast was clear, and Phaeton stepped into the car.

" I say," said one of the Dublin boys, " why don't you put up the stake before we start ? "

" The stake is all right," said Phaeton, just glancing over his shoulder at it.

" Who 's holding it ? " said the Dublin boy.

" Don't you see, the ground is holding it ? " said Phaeton, arranging the sand-bags.

" Oh, don't try to get out of it in that way," said the Dublin boy.

" I don't understand you," said Phaeton. " What do you mean ? "

" Did n't you say," said the Dublin boy, " you 'd give a dollar to any boy that could beat your machine in a mile run ? "

" No," said Phaeton. ' I have never said anything of the sort — nor thought of it. Who told you so ? "

" Lukey Finnerty."

" And who told Lukey Finnerty ? "

" Berny Rourke."

" And who told Berny Rourke ? "

" Teddy Dwyer."

" And who told Teddy Dwyer ? "

" Owney Geoghegan " (pronounced Gewgan).

" And who told Owney Geoghegan ? "

" Patsy Rafferty."

" And who told Patsy Rafferty ? "

" Oh, never mind who told me!" broke in another Dublin boy, who, it seems, was Patsy Rafferty. " The question is, are you going to put up the money ? "

" I never offered to put up any," said Phaeton. " And I have n't any with me, just now, to put up."

" Then somebody 's played us a trick," said Patsy.

" I'm sorry for that," said Phaeton.

" Ah, well, we don't mind—we 'll run all the same." said Patsy.

" But I don't care to have you run," said Phaeton. " In fact, I 'd rather you would n't."

" Well, we 're all ready for it," said Patsy, giving his trousers a hitch, and tightening the suspender a little by giving another twist to the nail that fastened it in lieu of a buckle. " And I suppose the road 's as free to us as 't is to you ? "

" Oh, certainly ! " said Phaeton.

"If you have n't any money," spoke up another Dublin boy, "you might say you 'll give a ride in your car to the fellow that beats it—just to lend a little interest to the race, you know."

Phaeton somewhat reluctantly said he would,—"although," he added, in an undertone, "if you can beat it, I don't see why you should want to ride in it."

Casting one more glance about, to see that all was ready, Phaeton told me to cut the rope and let him start. Partly because he spoke in a low tone, wishing to make as little excitement as possible, and partly because I was watching what I considered certain suspicious movements on the part of Monkey Roe, I did not hear or heed him.

"*Littera lapsa !*—let her slide !" roared out Holman, who saw that I had not understood.

With a quick, nervous stroke I drew the knife across the rope.

The machine started — at first with a little jerk, then with a slow rolling motion, gradually increasing in speed, until at the end of six or eight rods it was under rapid headway.

The Dublin boys at first stood still, looking on in gaping admiration at the wonder, till they suddenly remembered that they were there to race it, when they started off after it.

Our boys naturally followed them, as we could n't see any more of the fun unless we kept up with it.

It was a pretty even race, and all was going on smoothly, when down the first cross-street came a crowd of women, apparently very much excited, many of them with sticks in their hands. The sight of our moving crowd seemed to frenzy them, and they increased their speed, but only arrived at the corner in time to fall in behind us.

At the same time, down the cross-road from the other direction came a drove of cattle, pelted, pounded, and hooted at by two men and three boys; and close behind them was Dan Rice's Circus, which had been exhibiting for two days on the Falls Field, and was now hurrying on to the next town. Whether it was because of the red skirts worn by many of the women in front of them, or the rumbling of the circus so close behind them, I did not know, but those cattle did behave in the most frantic manner.

And so the whole caravan went roaring down the turnpike—Phaeton in his flying car at the head, then the Dublin boys, then our boys, then the mothers of the Dublin boys, then the drove of cattle, then the circus, with all its wagons and paraphernalia,—the striped zebra bringing up the rear.

It soon became evident that the mothers of the Dublin boys were proceeding on erroneous information — however they got it — and supposed that the contest between us and their sons was not a friendly one. For

"THE WHOLE CARAVAN WENT ROARING DOWN THE TURNPIKE."

whenever one of our boys lagged behind in the race, and came within reach of their sticks, he was pretty sure to get a sounding whack across the shoulders.   I dare say the Dublin boys would have received the same treatment if they had not been ahead of us in the race, which they always were, either because they were better runners, or better prepared.

Foremost of all was Patsy Rafferty, who, by doing his prettiest, had closed up the distance between himself and the car, and was now abreast of it.

Phaeton became excited, and, determined not to be beaten, lightened his car by hurriedly throwing out one of the bags of sand.   Unfortunately, it struck the ground right in front of Patsy, and the next instant he stubbed his toes on it and went sprawling into the gutter.

When the Dublin women saw this, they probably took it as full confirmation of the evil designs which somebody had told them we had on their sons, and some of our boys immediately paid the penalty by receiving a few extra whacks.

As for Patsy, he soon picked himself up and renewed the race, all the more determined to win it because he thought Phaeton had tripped him purposely—which I am happy to say was not true.

As we neared the railway crossing, Jack-in-the-Box was half way up the signal-pole. Hearing the outcry, he looked down upon us, took in the situation at a glance, then descended the pole two steps at a time, seized his red flag, and ran up the track at lightning speed. He had calculated that the Pacific express would arrive at the crossing just in time to dash through some part of our procession, and as he saw it would be useless to try to stop us, with everything crowding on behind us, he went to flag the train and stop that. This he just succeeded in doing, and when my section of the procession passed that given point,—you know it is the inveterate habit of processions to pass given points,—there stood the great locomotive stock still by Jack's box, with its train behind it, and seemed to look down upon us like an astonished and interested spectator.

We swept on across the track, and as there was a straight, smooth piece of road before us, all went well till we neared the canal. There a stupid fellow, as we afterward learned, leading home a cow he had just bought, had tied her to the corner-post of the bridge by which the turnpike crossed the canal, and gone into a neighboring grocery. The cow had placed herself directly across the narrow road-way of the bridge, and there she stood contentedly chewing her cud, entirely ignorant of the fact that an important race was in progress, and that she was obstructing the track.

Phaeton saw her with horror; for if he kept on, the car would run into her—the foot-path over the bridge was too narrow for it. He threw out his anchor, which ricochetted, as an artillerist would say.   That is, it would catch the ground for an instant, and then fly into the air, descend in a curve, catch again, and fly up again.   At last it caught on a horse-block, stuck fast, and brought the car to a stop.

But before Phaeton could climb out, Patsy Rafferty had come up, and, whipping out his jack-knife, cut the anchor-rope in two.   In an instant the machine was off again.

Phaeton's situation was desperate.   There stood the stupid cow like an animated toll-gate closing the bridge, and he rushing on to destruction at the rate of a good many miles an hour, with no way to stop the machine, and a certainty of broken bones if he jumped out.

In his agony, he half rose in the car and gave a terrific yell.   The cow started, saw him, and then clumsily but quickly swung herself around against the truss of the bridge that divided the carriage-way from the foot-path. But the carriage-way had been newly planked, and the planks were not yet nailed down.   As the cow stepped on the ends, four or five of these planks were instantly tilted up like a trap door, while the cow sank down till she was wedged between the truss and the first sleeper or lengthwise beam (the space being not quite large enough to let her drop through) ; the planks of course being held in an almost perpendicular position between her body and the sleeper.

Into the abyss that thus suddenly yawned before him, Phaeton and his chariot plunged.

After him went Patsy Rafferty, who on seeing the danger had laid hold of the car and tried to stop it, but failed. Whether he jumped through, or let himself down more cautiously by hanging from the floor of the bridge and dropping, I did not see ; but, at all events, when the rest of us reached the tow-path by running down the embankment, the waters of the canal had closed over both boys and the car.

At this moment another accident complicated the trouble and increased the excitement. This was a " tow-path bridge "—one which the boat-horses have to pass over, because at that point the tow-path changes from one side of the canal to the other. The " Red Bird " packet-horses, coming up at a round trot, when they reached the crown of the bridge and saw the rushing, roaring caravan coming at them, and heard Phaeton's yell, stopped, and stood shivering with fear. But the packet was all the while going ahead by its own momentum, and when it had gone the length of the tow-line, it jerked the horses over the parapet into the water, where they floundered within a yard of the sunken machine.

The Dublin women gathered on the tow-path, and immediately set up an unearthly wail, such as I have never heard before or since. I think that some of them must have " cried the keen," as it is called in Ireland.

Patsy soon emerged from beneath the wreck, hauling Phaeton out by the hair, and as half a dozen of the boys, from both parties, were now in the water, they had plenty of help. The bow-hand of the "Red Bird" cut the tow-line with a hatchet,—if he had been attending to his business, he would have done it soon enough to prevent the accident,—and the horses, thus released, swam ashore.

Meantime the circus had stopped, and many of the men came to the scene of the disaster, while most of the packet passengers stepped ashore and also joined the wondering crowd.

The steersman brought a long pike-pole, with which he fished out Phaeton's car.

Every one of the kite-strings was broken, and the kites had gone down the sky, with that wobbling motion peculiar to what the boys call a "kite-broke-away," to find lodgment in some distant forest or meadow.

Great was the wonderment expressed, and many were the questions asked, as the packet passengers and the circus people crowded around the rescued car and the dripping boys. The Dublin women were wringing out the jackets of our boys, and talking rather fast.

A benevolent-looking old gentleman, who wore a white vest and a large fob-chain, said, "Something ought to be done for that boy"—pointing to Patsy Rafferty.

The Clown of the circus said "Certainly!" and taking off his hat passed it first to the benevolent-looking old gentleman, who seemed a little surprised, but soon recovered, and hastily dropped in ten cents.

Then the Clown passed it all around, and nearly everybody, excepting the boys, of course, put in a little something. The Patagonian Woman of the circus, who had very red cheeks and very round eyes, and wore a large diamond ring on nearly every finger, gave the most of anybody,—half a dollar,—which she borrowed of the Strong Man, who used to lift the big iron balls on the back of his neck.

The Clown counted the money, and said there were three dollars and eighty-four cents, and a crossed shilling, and a bogus quarter, and two brass buttons, and a pewter temperance medal.

"Well," said he, in a solemn tone, looking down at the collection, and then around at the people, "I should say this crowd was about an average specimen of humanity."

I did n't see the Clown himself put in anything at all.

"Here, sonny," said he to Patsy, "we 'll tie it up in your handkerchief for you."

Patsy said he had n't any handkerchief with him, just then ; whereupon the Patagonian Woman gave him hers —excellent people, those Patagonians !—and the Clown tied it up with two hard knots, and Patsy tucked it into his trousers pocket, which it caused to bulge out as if he had just passed through 'Squire Higgins's orchard.

The boss of the circus offered to give Patsy a place, and take him right along, at fifteen dollars a month and his board.   Patsy was crazy to go ; but his mother said she could n't spare him.

Some of the circus men brought a pole and tackle from one of their wagons, and lifted the cow out of her uncomfortable position, after which they replaced the planks.

" All aboard ! " shouted the captain of the " Red Bird," for the tow-line had been mended and the horses rubbed down, and all the passengers started on a run for the boat, excepting the benevolent-looking old gentleman, who walked very leisurely, seeming to know it would wait for him.

" All aboard ! " shouted the boss of the circus, and his people climbed upon the wagons, whipped up the horses, and rumbled over the bridge.

The Dublin women each laid hold of one or more of their boys, and marched them home ; Lukey Finnerty's mother arguing, as they went along, that her boy had done as much as Patsy Rafferty, and got as wet, and therefore ought to have a share of the money.

" Oh, there's no doubt," said Mrs. Rafferty, in a gently sarcastic tone, " but your boy has taken in a great deal of cold water.   He shall have the temperance medal."

The other women promptly took up the question, some on Mrs. Finnerty's side and some on Mrs. Rafferty's, and thus, all talking at once, they passed out of sight.

CHAPTER IX.

THE ART DESERVATIVE.

WHEN Phaeton's kites went wobbling down the sky, Owney Geoghegan and three or four others of the Dublin boys who had escaped their mothers, started off on a chase for them. Phaeton, Ned, Holman, and I took the car up the bank, and when we arrived at the top we saw Monkey Roe walking away pretty rapidly.

"*Gravitas pro vehiculum!*—wait for the wagon!" shouted Holman to him.

Roe seemed a little uncertain whether to stop, but finally leaned against the fence and waited for us.

I observed that the drove of cattle had gone down to a shallow place in the canal on the other side of the bridge, and were most of them standing in the water, either drinking or contemplating. Their drivers were throwing stones at them, and saying uncomplimentary things, but they took it philosophically—which means they did n't mind it much. When you are stolidly indifferent to anything that ought to move you, your friends will say you take it philosophically.

"Was n't it an odd thing, Roe," said Holman, "that

all those Dublin boys should have got the idea that a prize was offered for anybody who could beat this machine ? "

" Yes, it was very odd," said Roe. " Fay, what sort of wood is this ? "

" Chestnut."

" But I say, Roe," continued Holman, " who in the world could have told them so ? "

" Probably somebody who was fond of a practical joke," said Roe. " Who did the blacksmith work for you, Fay ? "

" Fanning."

" And I suppose," persisted Holman, still talking to Roe, " that it must have been the same practical joker who sent their mothers after them."

" Very likely," said Roe. " Are you going to get the kites and harness her up again, Fay ? "

" Have n't made up my mind."

It was evident that Monkey Roe did n't want to talk about the mystery of the Dublin boys, and Holman — probably satisfied by this time that his suspicions were correct — himself changed the subject.

" When I saw this thing tearing down the turnpike," said he, " with all that rabble at its heels, and go splash into the canal, I was reminded of the story of Phaeton, which I had for my Latin lesson last week."

Of course, we asked him to tell the story.

"Phaeton," said Holman, "was a young scapegrace who was fond of fast horses, and thought there was nothing on four legs or any number of wheels that he could n't drive. His father was the Sun-god Helios—which is probably a corruption of 'Held a hoss' (I must ask Jack-in-the-Box about it)—and his mother's maiden name was Clymene—which you can easily see is only changed a little from 'climb-iny.' This shows how Phaeton came by his passion for climbing in the chariot and holding the hosses.

"One day, one of the boys, named Epaphus, tried to pick a quarrel with him by saying that he was not really a son of Helios, but was only adopted out of the poor-house. Phaeton felt pretty badly about it, for he did n't know but it might be true. So he went home as fast as he could, and asked Helios, right out plump, whether he was his own son, or only adopted out of the poor-house. 'Certainly,' said the old gentleman, 'you are my own son, and always have been, ever since you were born.'

"This satisfied Phaeton, but he was afraid it might not satisfy the boys who had heard Epaphus's remark. So he begged to be allowed to drive the chariot of the Sun one day, just to show people that he was his father's own boy. Helios shook his head. That was a very particular job; the chariot had to go out on time and come in on time, every day, and there could n't be any fooling about it. But the youngster hung on and teased so,

that at last his father told him he might drive just one
day, if he would never ask again."

" Did he have a gag-bit?" said Ned, remembering
his brother's remarks on the occasion of our brisk morning canter.

" Probably not," said Holman, " for gag-bits were
not then invented. The next morning old Helios gave
the boy all the instructions he could about the character
of the horses and the bad places in the road, and started
him off.

" He had n't gone very far when the team ran
away with him, and went banging along at a terrible rate,
knocking fixed stars out of their places, overturning and
scattering an immense pile of new ones that had been
corded up at the side of the road to dry (that 's what
makes the Milky Way), and at last setting the world on fire.

" Jupiter saw that something must be done, pretty
quick, too, so he threw a sand-bag, or a thunder-bolt, or
something of that sort, at him, and knocked over the
chariot, and the next minute it went plump into the river
Eridanus — which I 've no doubt is the Latin for Erie
Canal. You can easily see how it would come : Erie
canal — Erie ditch — Erie drain — Erie drainus — Eridanus.
That 's the way Professor Woodruff explains words to the
advanced class. He can tell you where any word came
from in two minutes.

" Phaeton was n't so lucky as you, Fay, for there was

no Patsy Rafferty to pull him out, and he was drowned, while his poor sisters stood on the tow-path and cried till they turned into poplar-trees."

We were all deeply interested in this remarkable story from Grecian mythology, told in good plain American, and from our report Holman was often called upon to repeat it to the other boys. It was this that gave Fayette Rogers the name of Phaeton.

The fate of the horizontal balloon for a time dampened Phaeton's ardor for invention, and he was willing at last to unite with Ned and me in an enterprise which promised to be more business-like than brilliant — the printing-office scheme.

Meanwhile, we had been doing what we could ourselves. The first necessity was a press. Ned, whom we considered a pretty good draughtsman, drew a plan for one, and he and I made it. There was nothing wrong about the plan ; it was strong and simple — two great virtues in any machine. But we constructed the whole thing of soft pine, the only wood that we could command, or that our tools would cut. Consequently, when we put on the pressure to print our first sheet — feeling as proud as if we were Faust, Gutenberg, Schöfer, the Elzevirs, Ben Franklin, and the whole Manutius family rolled into one — not only did the face of the types go into the paper, but the bottoms of them went right into the bed of the press.

"It acts more like a pile-driver than a printing-press," said Ned, ruefully.

"It 'll never do," said I. "We can't get along without Fay. When he makes a press, it will print."

"When Fay makes a press," said Ned, "he 'll probably hire somebody else to make it. But I guess that 's the sensible way. I suppose the boys would laugh at

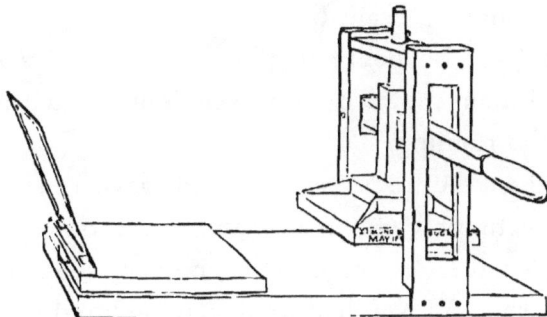

NED'S PLAN FOR A PRESS.

this thing, even if it worked well; it looks so dreadfully cheese-pressy."

"It does look a little that way," said I. "But Fay will get up something handsome, and I've no doubt we can find some good use for this — perhaps keep it in the corner for the boys to fool with when they call. They 'll be certain to meddle with something, and this may keep their hands from the good one."

"I don't intend to run the office on any such principles," said Ned. "The boy that meddles with anything will be invited to leave."

"Then you'll make them all angry, and there wont be any good-will to it," said I. "I've heard Father say that the good-will of the *Vindicator* office was worth more than all the type and presses. He says the *Vindicator* lives on its good-will."

"That may be all very nice for the *Vindicator*," said Ned; "but this office will have to live on hard work."

"But we must be polite to the boys that patronize the establishment," said I.

"Oh, yes; be polite to them, of course," said Ned. "But tell them they've got to keep out of our way when the press is running."

Whether the press ever would have run, or even crawled, without Phaeton to manage it, is doubtful. But he now joined in the enterprise, and very soon organized the concern. As Ned had predicted, he hired a man who was a carriage-maker by trade, but had a genius for odd jobs, to make us a press. In those days, the small iron presses which are now manufactured in great numbers, and sold to boys throughout the country, had not been heard of. Ours was a pretty good one, made partly of wood and partly of iron, with a powerful knee-joint, which gave a good impression. The money to pay for it came from Aunt Mercy *via* Ned.

There was a small, unused building in our yard, about fifteen feet square, sometimes called the "wash-house," and sometimes "the summer-kitchen," now abandoned and almost empty. Phaeton, looking about for a place for the proposed printing-office, fixed upon this as the very thing that was wanted. He said it could not have been better if it had been built on purpose.

After some negotiation with my parents, their consent was obtained, and Phaeton and Ned took me into partnership, I furnishing the building, and they furnishing the press and type. We agreed that the name of the firm should be Rogers & Co. On the gable of the office we erected a short flag-staff, cut to the form of a printer's "shooting-stick," and whenever the boys saw the Stars and Stripes floating from it, they knew the office was open for business.

"This font of Tuscan," said Ned to Phaeton, as we were putting the office in order, "is not going to be so useless as you suppose, even if the Es are all gone."

"How so?" said Phaeton.

"Because I asked a printer about it, and he says when you find a box empty you simply use some other letter in place of the one that is missing—generally X. And here are plenty of Xs."

Phaeton only smiled, and went on distributing type into his case of pica.

"I say, Fay," said Ned again, after a while, "don't you think it would be proper to do a little something for Patsy Rafferty, just to show your gratitude for his services in pulling you out of the canal?"

6

" I 've thought about it," said Phaeton.

" We might print him a dozen cards, with his name on," said Ned, " and not charge him a cent. Get them up real stylish — red ink, perhaps ; or Patsy in black and Rafferty in red ; something that 'll please him." And Ned immediately set up the name in Tuscan, to see how it would look. It looked like this :

MR. PATSY RAFFXRTY, XSQ.

" How do you think he 'd like that, done in two colors ? " said Ned.

" I don't believe he 'd care much about it," said Phaeton. " But I 've invited him to come over here this afternoon, and perhaps we can find out what he would like."

Patsy came in the afternoon, and was made acquainted with some of the mysteries of printing. After a while, Ned showed him what he intended to print on a dozen cards for him.

" It 's very nice, indeed," said Patsy ; " but that 's not my name."

" Not your name ? " said Ned.

" No," said Patsy. " My father's name is Mr. Patsy Rafferty, Esquire ; but I 'm only Patsy Rafferty, without any handle or tail to it."

" If that's all that ails it," said Ned, " it's easy enough to take off the handle and tail," and he took them off.

Patsy took another look at it.

"That's not exactly the way I spell my name," said he. "There ought to be an E there, instead of an X."

"Of course there ought," said Ned, "but you see we have n't any Es in that style of type, and it 's an old established rule in all printing-offices that when there 's a letter you have n't got, you simply put an X in place of it. Everybody understands it."

"I did n't understand it," said Patsy, "and I think my name looks better when it's spelled the way I was christened."

"All right!" said Ned. "We 'll make it as you want it; but it 'll have to be set in some other kind of type, and that Tuscan is the prettiest thing in the office."

Patsy still preferred correctness to beauty, and had his way.

"And now what color will you have?" said Ned. "We can print it in black, or red, or blue, or partly one color and partly another — almost any color, in fact."

Patsy, true to the tradition of his ancestors, chose green.

"I'm awful sorry," said Ned, "but we have n't any green ink. It's about the only color we have n't got."

"You can make it by mixing blue and yellow together," said Patsy.

"True," said Ned; "but the fact is, we have n't any yellow. Green and yellow are about the only colors we have n't got."

After studying the problem a few minutes, Patsy chose to have his visiting-cards printed in alternate red and blue letters, and we set about it at once, Ned arranging the type, while I took the part of devil and managed the ink. As they were to be in two colors, of course each card had to go through the press twice ; and they were not very accurately "registered," as a printer would say—that is, the red letters, instead of coming exactly on even spaces between the blue, would sometimes be too far one way, sometimes too far the other, sometimes even lapping over the blue letters. But out of fifty or sixty that we printed, Patsy selected thirteen that he thought would do—"a dozen, and one for luck"— and, without waiting for them to dry, packed them together and put them into his pocket, expressing his own admiration and anticipating his mother's. He even intimated that when she saw those she would probably order some for herself.

Patsy asked about Phaeton's chariot, and whether it was hurt much when it went into the canal.

"Hardly damaged at all," said Phaeton.

Patsy hinted that he would like to see it, and he and Phaeton went over to Rogers's. When Phaeton returned an hour later, he was alone.

"Where's Patsy?" said Ned.

"Gone home with the chariot," said Phaeton.

"Gone home with the chariot?" said Ned, in astonishment.

"Yes," said Phaeton, "I have given it to him. I saw, by the way he looked at it and talked about it, that it would be a great prize to him, and I did n't intend to use it any more myself, so I made him a present of it."

"But you had no right to," said Ned. "That chariot was built with my money."

"Not exactly," said Phaeton. "It was built with money that I borrowed of you. I still owe you the money, but the car was mine."

"Well, at any rate," said Ned, who saw this point clearly enough, "you might have sold the iron on it for enough to buy another font of type."

"Yes, I might," said Phaeton. "But I preferred giving it to Patsy. He 's a good deal of a boy, and I hope Father wont forget that he said he should do something for him."

"But what use will the car be to him?" said Ned.

"He says it 'll be a glorious thing to slide down hill in summer," said Phaeton.

A few days afterward, Patsy came again to see Phaeton, and wanted to know if he could not invent some means by which the car could be prevented from going down hill too fast. He said that when Berny Rourke and Lukey Finnerty and he took their first ride in it, down one of the long, grassy slopes that bordered the Deep Hollow, it went swifter, and swifter, until it reached the edge of the brook, where it struck a lump of sod and threw them all into the water.

"Water is an excellent thing," said Ned, "for a sudden stoppage of a swift ride. They always use it in horizontal balloon-ascensions, and on the Underground Railroad they 're going to build all the depots of it."

Phaeton, who appeared to be thinking deeply, only smiled, and said nothing. At last he exclaimed:

"I have it, Patsy! Come with me."

They went off together, and Phaeton hunted up an old boot, the leg of which he drove full of shingle-nails, driving them from the inside outward. Then he filled it with stones and sand, and sewed the top together. Then he found a piece of rope, and tied one end to the straps.

"There, Patsy," said he, "tie the other end of the rope to one of the hooks on the car, and take the boot in with you. When you are going fast enough, throw it out for a drag. I don't believe a streak of lightning could make very good headway, if it had to pull that thing along on the ground after it."

Patsy, Berny, and Lukey tried it, but were thrown into the brook as before. Phaeton said the true remedy was, more old boots; and they added one after another, till they had a cluster of seven, which acted as an effectual drag, and completely tamed the spirit of the machine, after which it soon became the most popular institution in Dublin. Patsy said seven was one of the lucky numbers.

To return to the printing business. When I was

about to sit down at the tea-table, that evening, Mother exclaimed :

"What in the world ails your hands?"

I looked at them. Some of my fingers were more red than blue, some were more blue than red, and some about equally red and blue. I said I guessed Patsy Rafferty's visiting-cards were what ailed my hands.

"Well, I wish you'd wash your hands of Patsy Rafferty's visiting-cards," said she.

"Can't do it with any such slimpsy water as we have here," said I.

"And where do they have any that is less slimpsy?" said Mother.

"At the printing-offices," said I. "They put a little ley in it. We have n't any at our office, but that's the next thing we're going to buy. Don't worry; it wont rub off on the bread and butter, and we shall have a can of ley next week."

"The next thing to be done," said Ned, when we had the office fairly in running order, "is to get up a first-rate business-card of our own, have it large enough, print it in colors, and make a stunning thing of it."

"That reminds me," said Phaeton, "that I was talking with Jack-in-the-Box about our office the other day, and I told him we ought to have a pretty poetical motto to put up over the door. He suggested two or three, and wrote them down for me. Perhaps one of them would look well on the card."

" What are they ? " said Ned.

After some searching, Phaeton found a crumpled piece of paper in one of his pockets, and smoothing it out showed the following, hastily scratched in pencil :

> Faith, he 'll prent it.—*Burns.*
>
> I have misused the king's press.—*Shakespeare.*
>
> So careful of the type she seems.—*Tennyson.*

" I don't like one of them," said Ned.

" Why not ? " said Phaeton.

" Well, the first one is spelled wrong. We *print* here, we don't *prent*."

" But it means the same thing," said Phaeton; "that 's the Scotch of it. Burns was a Scotchman."

" Was he ? " said Ned. " Well, I never heard of him before, and we don't want any of his Scotch spelling. That second motto is all wrong; the press belongs to us, not to any king, and we 're not going to misuse it. The third one would do pretty well, but it says ' she,' and we 're none of us girls."

" Perhaps you can think of a better one," said Phaeton.

" Yes, I can," said Ned. " I heard Uncle Hiram say that printing was called the art deservative of all arts, and that would be just the motto for us."

" What does it mean ? " said I.

" It means," said Ned, " that printers deserve more than any other artists."

" Did n't he say *pre*servative ? " said Phaeton.

" Oh, no," said Ned; " that would n't mean anything. Printing has nothing to do with preserving—unless we should print the labels for Mother's fruit-cans next fall. He said 'deservative,' I heard him distinctly, and we'll put it on the card."

"Very well," said Phaeton; "you set up the card according to your own taste, and we'll see how we like it."

The next day Phaeton and I went fishing. While we were gone Ned set up the card, and on our return we found, to our consternation, that he had not only set it up, but printed scores of them, and given away a good many to the boys. It ran as follows:

" The Aʌt Deservitive of al Arts."

ROGERS & CO.

GOB PRINTERS,

At the Seign of the Shootinɓ Stick.

cards	books
posters	doggers
leter heads	handbils
bill heads	programes,&c.

The undesigned are prepaired to exicute all kinps of Gob Printing on short notice, and in the most artistic maner.

Call and sxx our xstablishmxnt!

Visitors are wellcome, and will be showed through the works by a poalite attendant.

N. B. The Pen is miɜhtyer than the Swoard.

6*

" Good gracious, Ned ! " said Phaeton, " why did you print this thing before we had seen it ? "

" Because I felt sure you 'd like it," said Ned, " and I wanted to surprise you."

" You 've succeeded admirably in that," said Phaeton.

" I hope there 's nothing wrong about it," said Ned. " I took a great deal of pains with it. Oh, yes ; now I see there 's one letter upside down. But what of that ? Very few people will notice it, and they will know it 's an accident."

" One ? " said Phaeton. " There are half a dozen standing on their heads. And that 's not the worst. Just look at the spelling ! "

" I don't see anything wrong about that," said Ned. " You must remember that what 's wrong by Webster may be right by Worcester."

" What do you call that ? " said Phaeton, pointing at the first word in the third line.

" Job, of course," said Ned. " Some people spell it with a J, but that can't be right. J-o-b spells Job, the name of that king of Israel who had so many boils on him at once."

" He was n't king of Israel," said Phaeton.

" Well, king of Judah, then," said Ned. " I always get those two mixed. What 's the use of being too particular. Those old kings are as dead now as Julia Cæsar. And everybody knows how dead she is."

"Well, then, what's this?" said Phaeton, pointing to the second word on the right-hand side of the press.

"Don't you know what dodgers are?" said Ned. "Little bills with 'Bankrupt Sale!' or 'Great Excitement!' or something of that sort across the top, to throw around in the yards, or hand to the people coming out of church."

"Oh, yes; dodgers," said Phaeton. "But I never saw it spelled so before. Have you given out many of these cards?"

"I gave one to Holman," said Ned, "and one to Monkey Roe, and one to Jack-in-the-Box."

"What did Jack-in-the-Box say to it?" said Phaeton.

"Oh, he admired it amazingly," said Ned. "He said it was the most entertaining business-card he had ever seen. But he thought perhaps it would be well for us to have a proof-reader. I asked him what that was, and he said it was a round-shouldered man, with a green shade over his eyes, who knew everything. He sits in the corner of your office, and when you print anything he reads the first one and marks the mistakes on it, so that you can correct them before you print any more. We might get Jimmy the Rhymer; he's awful round-shouldered, but he does n't know everything. The only man in this town who knows everything is Jack-in-the-Box himself, and I suppose we could n't get him."

"I suppose not," said Phaeton, "though I know he'd

look over a proof for us, any time we took one to him. But now tell me whether you 've given out any more of these cards."

"Well, yes, a few," said Ned. "Patsy Rafferty was over here; he rolled for me, or I could n't have got them done so soon; and when he went home, he took fifty to leave at the doors of the houses on his way. I thought if we were going to do business, it was time to be letting people know about it."

"Just so," said Phaeton. "And is that all?"

"Not quite. Uncle Jacob was going to ride out to Parma, and I gave him about forty, and asked him to hand them to people he met on the road."

"Y-e-s," said Phaeton, with a deep sigh; "and is *that* all?"

"I put a dozen or two on that little shelf by the post-office window," said Ned, "so that anybody who came for his letters could take one. And now that 's all; and I hope you wont worry over one or two little mistakes. Everybody makes some mistakes. There is no use in pretending to be perfect. But if you two fellows had been here in the office, instead of going off to enjoy yourselves fishing and leaving me to do all the work, you might have had the old card just as you wanted it. Of course you 'd have spelled it right, but there might have been bad taste about it that would look worse than my spelling. And now I 'm going home to supper."

" The worst thing about Ned," said Phaeton, after he had gone, " is, that there 's too much go-ahead in him. Very few people are troubled in that way."

" But what are we going to do about that dreadful card ? " said I. " When the people see that, they may be afraid to give us any jobs, for fear that we 'll misspell everything."

" I don't know what we can do now," said Phaeton, " unless we get out a good one, and say on it that no others are genuine. I must think about it over night."

CHAPTER X.

IN spite of Ned's declaration that he would tolerate no loungers, the office soon became a favorite gathering-place for the boys of the neighborhood; which fact contributed nothing to the speed or accuracy of the work. They made us a great deal of trouble at first, for few of them knew better than to take a type out of one box, examine it curiously, and throw it into another; or lift a page of type that had just been set up, "to see how heavy it was," and let it drop into a mass of pi. They got over this after a while, but they never did quite get over the habit of discussing all sorts of questions in a loud voice; and sometimes, when we happened to be setting type, and were interested in what they were talking about, fragments of the conversation would mingle in our minds with the copy before us, and the curious effect would horrify us in the proof.

For instance, Monkey Roe's mother had employed us to print her a few copies of Mrs. Opie's poem, "The Orphan Boy," which she had known since she was a child, and very greatly admired, but of which she had

never had any but a manuscript copy. While I was setting it up, three boys were carrying on an animated discussion about the city fire department, and when I took a
proof of my work, I found it read like this :

Stay, lady, stay, for mercy's sake,
And hear the Brick Church bell strike the 4th District.
Ah ! sure my looks must pity no by crackie Orph Bo
Cataract Eight can't begin to throw the stream Red
Rover Three can — Tis want that makes Reliance Five
wash my cheek so pale at annual inspection.

Yet I was once a mother's pride, Three's men cut her
hose at the Orchard street fire before Bix Six's air chamber busted my brave father's hope and joy.

But in the Nile's proud fight he sucked Archer's well
dry in three minutes and a half, and I am now Assistant
Foreman of Torrent Two with a patent brake on the
Orphan Boy.

I am afraid if Monkey's mother had seen that, she
would hardly have recognized it as the first stanza of her
favorite poem. Instead of feeling sorry for spoiling my
work, the boys seemed to think it was a good joke, and
nearly laughed their heads off over it. They insisted on
my printing a few copies of it, just as it was, for them to
keep. Next time I saw Jack-in-the-Box, he showed me
one of them pasted into a little old scrap-book that he

kept under his chair. On the opposite page was one of our business-cards, as printed by Ned. Jack very kindly explained to me some of the mysteries of proof-reading.

"The next thing to be done," said Ned, when the office was fairly in running order, "is to get out Jimmy the Rhymer's poems. That's what we got up the establishment for, and it'll be more profitable than all these little puttering jobs put together. And, besides, Jimmy's awful poor and needs the money. I've been around to the book-stores and told them about it. Hamilton promises to take ten copies, and Hoyt twenty-five. When they see how good the poems are, they'll be sure to double their orders; and when the other stores see the book going off like hot cakes, they'll rush in and want to buy some, but they'll have to wait their turn. First come, first served."

There were enough of Jimmy's poems to make a little book of about sixty pages, and we all went to work with a will to set the type. It would have been a pretty long job for us, as it was, but Jimmy made it a great deal longer, and nearly drove us crazy, by insisting on making changes in them after they were set up. He could not understand how much extra work this made for us, and was as particular and persistent as if his whole reputation as an author had hung on each disputed comma. Sometimes when we had four pages all ready to print, he would bring in a new stanza, to be inserted in the first page of the form, which, of course, made it necessary to change the arrangement of all the others. At last Ned got out of patience.

"You try it yourself once," said he to Jimmy, "and you 'll find out whether it's easy to make all these little changes, as you call them."

Jimmy secretly made up his mind that he would try it himself. He went to the office one day when we were not there, found four pages "locked up" ready for print-

THE MEDDLESOME POET.

ing, and went to work to make a few corrections. As he

did not know how to unlock the form, he stood it up on edge, got a ten-penny nail and a mallet, and tried to knock out an obnoxious semicolon.

The result was a sudden bursting of the form, which rattled down into ruin at his feet, and frightened the meddlesome poet out of his wits.

In his bewilderment, Jimmy scooped up a double handful of the pi and was in the act of pouring it pell-mell into one of the cases, when Phaeton, Ned, and I arrived at the door of the office.

Ned, who saw him first, and instantly comprehended the situation, gave a terrific yell, which caused Jimmy to drop the handful of type, some of which went into the case, and the rest spattered over the floor.

"Are you trying to ruin the office?" said Ned. "Don't you know better than to pi a form, and then throw the pi into the cases? After all the trouble we've had with your old poems, you ought to have more gratitude than that."

Jimmy was pale with terror, and utterly dumb.

"Hold on, Ned," said Phaeton, laying his hand on his brother's shoulder. "You ought to have sense enough to know that it must have been an accident of some sort. Of course Jimmy would n't do it purposely."

"Pieing the form may have been an accident," said Ned; "but when he scoops up a double handful of the pi and goes to pouring it into the case, that can't be an accident. And it was my case, too, and I was the one that did everything for him, and was going to bring him out as a poet in the world's history. If he had behaved himself, I'd have set him up in business in a little while, so he could have made as much money as Sir Walter Tupper, or any of those other fellows that you read to us about. And now, just look at that case of mine, with probably every letter of the alphabet in every box of it."

"But I tell you it must have been a mere accident," said Phaeton. "Was n't it, Jimmy?"

"Suppose it was an accident," said Ned; "the question is, *whose* accident was it? If it had been my accident, I should expect to pay for it."

Phaeton took hold of his brother's arm with a quiet but powerful grasp, and led him to the door.

"You 're needlessly excited, Ned," said he. "Go outside till you get cooled off." And he put him out and shut the door.

Then he asked Jimmy how it happened, and Jimmy told us about it.

"I 'm sorry you poured any of it in the cases," said Phaeton. "For, you see, the cases have a different letter in every box, and if you take a handful of type like that and pour it in at random, it makes considerable trouble."

"Oh, yes; I knew all that before," said Jimmy; "but when the form burst, and I saw the type all in a mess on the floor, I was so frightened I lost my head, and did n't know what I was about. I wish I could pay for it," he added, as he left the office.

" Don't let it trouble you," said Phaeton.

For a long time Jimmy did not come near us again, and as he had carried off the copy of his remaining poems, that enterprise came to an end—for the time being, at least.

There was no lack of other jobs, but we sometimes had a little trouble in collecting the bills. Small boys would keep coming to order visiting-cards by the hundred, with their name on them in ornamental letters,— boys who never used any visiting-card but a long, low whistle, and never had a cent of money except on Fourth of July. When Phaeton or I was there, they were given to understand that a pressure of other work compelled us to decline theirs with regret ; but, if they found Ned alone, they generally persuaded him that they had good prospects of getting money from some source or other, and so went away with the cards in their pockets.

There was no lack of advice, either. The boys who lounged in the office were always proposing new schemes. The favorite one seemed to be the publication of a small paper, which some of them promised to write for, others to get advertisements for, and others to distribute. After the book of poems had come to an untimely end, Ned was fierce for going into the paper scheme; but Phaeton figured it up, declared we should have to do an immense amount of work for about a cent an hour, and put an effectual veto on the plan.

Charlie Garrison, who, while the other boys only lounged and gossiped, "learned the case," and quietly picked up a good deal of knowledge of the trade, intimated one day that he would like to be taken into the partnership.

"Yes," said Ned; "there's work enough here for another man; but you'd have to put in some capital, you know."

"Put in capitals wherever they belong, of course," said Charlie; "begin proper names and every line of poetry."

"I mean money," said Ned. "Money's called capital, you know, when it's put into business. We put capital into this office, and you'd have to, if we took you into partnership."

"Oh, that's it," said Charlie, musingly. "Well, I suppose I could; we live on the Bowl System at our house; but I should hardly like to take it."

"The Bowl System? What's that?" said Ned. "Soup, or bread-and-milk, for every meal?"

"No; not that at all," said Charlie. "You see, on the highest shelf in our pantry there's a two-quart bowl, with a blue-and-gold rim around it. Whenever any member of the family gets any money, he puts it into that bowl; and whenever any of us want any money, we take it out of that bowl. I've seen the bowl full of money, and I've seen it when it had only five cents in it. The fullest I ever saw it was just before sister Edith was married. For a long time they all kept putting in as much as they could, and hardly took out anything at all, till the bowl got so full that the money slid off from the top. Then they took it all out, and went down town and bought her wedding things. And oh, you ought to have seen them! Stacks and stacks of clothes that I don't even know the names of."

"Then I suppose you could help yourself to all the capital you want, out of the bowl?" said Ned.

"Yes, I could," said Charlie; "but I should n't like to; for I am the only one of the family that never puts anything into it. Perhaps other people don't know it by that name, but brother George calls it living on the Bowl System."

"Why don't you put the money into the bank?" said Phaeton.

"Father had a lot of money in a bank once," said Charley, "but the bank broke, and he said he'd never put in any more."

"I wish we lived on the Bowl System at our house," said Monkey Roe. "It would n't be many days before I'd have a velocipede and a double-barrelled pistol."

CHAPTER XI.

THE business of the printing-office went on pretty steadily, so far as Ned and I were concerned. Phaeton's passion for invention would occasionally lead him off for a while into some other enterprise; yet he, too, seemed to take a steady interest in " the art deservative." The most notable of those enterprises was originated by Monkey Roe, who had considerable invention, but lacked Phaeton's powers of execution.

One day Monkey came to the door of the office with Mitchell's " Astronomy " in his hand, and called out Phaeton

" There's some mischief on foot now," said Ned; " and if Fay goes off fooling with any of Monkey Roe's schemes, we shall hardly be able to print the two thousand milk-tickets that John Spencer ordered yesterday. It's too bad."

When they had gone so far from the office that we could not hear their conversation, I saw Monkey open the book and point out something to Phaeton. They appeared to carry on an earnest discussion for several minutes, after which they laid the book on the railing of the fence and disappeared, going by the postern.

Ned ran out, and brought in the book. On looking it over, we found a leaf turned down at the chapter on comets. Neither of us had studied astronomy.

"I know what they're up to," said Ned, after taking a long look at a picture of Halley's comet. "I heard the other day that Mr. Roe was learning the art of stuffing birds. I suppose Monkey wants Fay to help him shoot one of those things, or catch it alive, may be, and sell it to his father."

Then I took a look at the picture, and read a few lines of the text.

"I don't think it's quite fair in Fay," continued Ned, "to go off on speculations of that sort for himself alone, and leave us here to do all the work in the office, when he has an equal share of our profits."

"Ned," said I, "I don't believe this is a bird."

"Well, then, it's a fish," said Ned, who had gone back to his case and was setting type. "They stuff fishes, as well as birds."

"But it seems to me it can hardly be a fish," said I, after another look.

"Why not?"

"Because I don't see any fins."

"That's nothing," said Ned. "My book of natural history says a fish's tail is a big fin. And I'm sure that fellow has tail enough to get along very well without any other fins."

This did not satisfy me, and at length we agreed to go and consult Jack-in-the-Box about it.

"Jack," said Ned, as soon as we arrived at the Box, "did you ever stuff a fish?"

"Do you take me for a cook?" said Jack, looking considerably puzzled.

"I don't mean a fish to bake," said Ned. "I mean one to be put in a glass case, and kept in a museum."

"Oh," said Jack, "I beg pardon. I did n't understand. No, I never stuffed a fish."

"But, I suppose you know all about how it 's done?" said Ned.

"Oh, yes; I understand it in a general way."

"What I want to get at," said Ned, "is this: how much is a fish worth that 's suitable for stuffing?"

"I don't know exactly," said Jack, "but I should say different ones would probably bring different prices, according to their rarity."

"That sounds reasonable," said Ned. "Now, how much should you say a fellow would probably get for one of this sort?" and he opened the Astronomy at the picture of Halley's comet.

"Something was the matter with Jack's face. It twitched around in all sorts of ways, and his eyes sparkled with a kind of electric light. But he passed his hand

7

over his features, took a second look at the picture, and answered :

"If you can catch one of those, I should say it would command a very high price."

"So I thought," said Ned. "Should you say as much as a hundred dollars, Jack ? "

" I should not hesitate to say fully two hundred," said Jack, as he took his flag and went out doors to signal a freight-train.

" I see it all, as plain as day," said Ned to me, as we walked away. " Fay has gone off to make a lot of money by what father would call an outside speculation, and left us to dig away at the work in the office."

" Perhaps he 'll go shares with us," said I.

" No, he wont," said Ned. " But I have an idea. I think I can take a hand in that speculation."

" How will you do it ? "

" I 'll offer Fay and Monkey a hundred dollars for their fish, if they catch it. That 'll seem such a big price, they 'll be sure to take it. And then I 'll sell it for two hundred, as Jack says. So I 'll make as much money as both of them together. And I must give Jack a handsome present for telling me about it."

" That seems to be a good plan," said I. " And I hope they 'll catch two, so that I can buy one and specu- late on it. But, then," I added, sorrowfully, " I have n't the hundred dollars to pay for it, and there 's no Aunt

Mercy in our family, and we don't live on the Bowl System."

"Never mind," said Ned, in a comforting tone. "Perhaps you'll inherit a big fortune from some old grandmother you never heard of, till she died and they ripped open her bed-tick and let the gold tumble out. Lots of people do."

As we arrived home, we saw Phaeton and Monkey coming by the postern with half a dozen hoops — that is to say, half a dozen long, thin strips of ash, which would have been hoops after the cooper had bent them into circles and fastened the ends together.

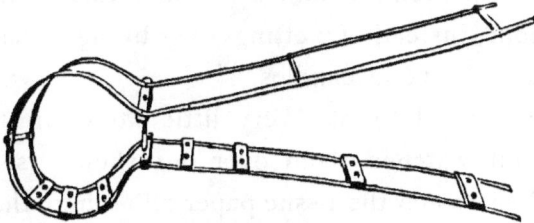

THE FRAME.

"That's poor stuff to make fish-poles," said Ned, in a whisper; "but don't let them know that we know what they're up to."

They brought them into the office, got some other pieces of wood, and went to work constructing a light frame about ten feet long, three feet high at the highest part, and a foot wide — like that shown in the engraving.

"What are you making, Fay?" said Ned.

"Wait a while, and you'll see," said Phaeton.

Ned winked at me in a knowing way, and we went on printing milk-tickets.

When the frame was completed, Monkey and Phaeton went away.

"I see," whispered Ned. "They're going to catch him with a net. The netting will be fastened on all around here, and this big end left open for him to go in. Then, when he gets down to this round part, he'll find he can't go any farther, and then they'll haul him up. It's all as plain as day."

But when Monkey and Phaeton returned, in about half an hour, instead of netting they brought yellow tissue-paper and several candles.

We pretended to take very little interest in the proceeding, but watched them over our shoulders. When we saw them fasten the tissue-paper all around the frame, except on the top, and fit the candles into auger-holes bored in the cross-pieces at the bottom, Ned whispered to me again:

"Don't you see? That isn't a net. They're going to have a light in it, and carry it along the shore to attract the fish. It's plain enough now."

"If you'll be on hand to-night," said Monkey, "and follow us, you may see some fun."

"All right! We'll be on hand," said Ned and I.

In the evening we all met in the office — all except Phaeton, who was a little late.

"Monkey," said Ned, in a confidential tone, "I want to make you an offer."

"Offer away," answered Monkey.

"If you catch one," said Ned, "I'll give you a hundred dollars for it."

"If I catch one?" said Monkey. "If — I — catch — one? Oh, yes — all right! I'll give you whatever I catch, for that price. Though I may not catch anything but Hail Columbia."

"But I won't take it unless it's the kind they stuff," said Ned.

"The kind—they—stuff?" said Monkey. "Did you say the kind *they* stuff, or the kind *of* stuff? Oh, yes — the kind of Hail Columbia they stuff. That would be a bald eagle, I should think."

At this moment Phaeton joined us.

"It's no use, Fay," said Monkey. "Jack wont let us hoist it on the signal-pole. He says it might mislead some of the engineers, and work mischief."

"Hoist it on the signal-pole," whispered Ned to me. "Then it's a bird they're going to catch, after all, and not a fish. I see it now. Probably some wonderful kind of night-hawk."

"Well, then, what do you think is the next best place?" said Phaeton.

"I think Haven's barn, by all odds," Monkey answered promptly.

"Haven's barn it is, then," said Phaeton, and they shouldered the thing and walked off, we following.

Before we arrived at the barn, Holman, Charlie Garrison, and at least a dozen other boys had joined us, one by one.

The numerous ells and sheds attached to this barn enabled Monkey and Phaeton to mount easily to the ridgepole of the highest part, where they fastened the monster, and quickly lighted all her battle-lanterns, when she blazed out against the blackness of the night like some terrific portent.

"Now you stay here and keep her in order," said Monkey, "while I go for Adams."

Mr. Adams was an amateur astronomer of considerable local celebrity, whose little observatory, built by himself, was about fifty rods distant from Haven's barn. Unfortunately, his convivial habits were as famous as his scientific attainments, and Roe knew about where to find him. I went with him on the search.

We went first to the bar-room of the "Cataract House, by James Tone," but we did not find him there.

"Then," said Roe, "I know where he is, for sure," and he went to a dingy, wooden building on State street, which had small windows with red curtains. This building was ornamented with a poetical sign, which every boy

in town knew by heart, and could sing to the tune of
" Oats, peas, beans."

W. WHEELER KEEPS IN HERE,
SELLS GROCERIES, CIDER, ALE, AND BEER ;
HIS PRODUCE IS GOOD, HIS WEIGHT IS JUST,
HIS PROFITS SMALL, AND CANNOT TRUST ;
AND THOSE WHO BUY SHALL BE WELL USED,
SHALL NOT BE CHEATED, NOR ABUSED.

" Is Professor Adams present ? " said Monkey, as he
opened the door and peered through a cloud of tobacco
smoke.

An individual behind the stove returned a drowsy af-
firmative.

Roe stepped around to him, and with a great show of
secrecy whispered something in his ear.

He sprang from his chair, exclaimed, " Good night,
gentlemen ! You will wake up to-morrow morning to find
me famous," and dashed out at the door.

" What is it ? " said one of the loungers, detaining
Monkey as he was about to leave.

" A comet," whispered Monkey.

" A comet, gentlemen — a blazing comet ! " repeated
the man aloud ; and the whole company rose and followed
the astronomer to his observatory. When they arrived
there, they found him sitting with his eye at the instru-

ment, uttering exclamations of thankfulness that he had lived to make this great discovery.

"Not Biela's, not Newton's, not Encke's—not a bit like any of them," said he; "all my own, gentlemen—entirely my own!"

Then he took up his slate, and went to figuring upon it. Several of the crowd, who were now jammed close together around him in the little octagonal room, made generous offers of assistance.

"I was always good at the multiplication-table," said one of them.

"I have a fine, clear eye," said another; "can't I help yez aim the pipe?"

This excited a laugh of derision from another, who inquired whether the man with the fine, clear eye "did n't know a pipe from a chube?"

Another rolled up his sleeves, and said he was ready to take his turn at the crank for the cause of science; while still another expressed his willingness to blow the bellows all night, if Professor Adams would show him where the handle was.

They all insisted on having a peep at the comet through the telescope, and with some jostling took turns about.

One man, after taking a look, murmured solemnly:

"That thing bodes no good to this city; I'm going home to make my will," and elbowed his way out of the room.

"A COMET, GENTLEMEN—A BLAZING COMET!"

"Ah, Professor," said another, "your fortune's made for all time. This'll be known to fame as the Great American Comet. I dare say it's as big as all the comets of the old world put together."

Mr. Wheeler took an unusually long look.

"Gentlemen," said he, "I don't believe that comet will stay with us long. We'd better leave the Professor to his calculations, while we go back and have a toast to his great discovery."

But nobody stirred. Then Mr. Wheeler left the observatory, and walked straight up to Haven's barn. He picked up a cart-stake, swung it around his head, and hurled it; and, in the twinkling of an eye, that comet had passed its perihelion, and shot from the solar system in so long an ellipse that I fear it will never return.

Unfortunately, the flying cart-stake not only put out the comet, but struck Phaeton, who had been left there by Monkey Roe to manage the thing, and put his arm out of joint. He bore it heroically, and climbed down to the ground alone before he told us what had happened. Then, as he nearly fainted away, we helped him home, while Holman ran for the family physician, who arrived in a few minutes and set the arm.

"It serves me right," said Phaeton, "for ever lending myself to any of Monkey Roe's schemes to build a mere fool-thing.

"I'm sorry you're hurt," said Ned; "but it does

seem as if that comet was a silly machine, only intended to deceive me and Professor Adams, instead of being for the good of mankind, like your other inventions. And now you won't be able to do anything in the printing-office for a long while, just when we 're crowded with work. If you were not my own brother, and such an awful good fellow, we would n't let you have any share of the profits for the next month."

CHAPTER XII.

THE printing-office enjoyed a steady run of custom, and, as Ned had said, we were just now crowded with work. Almost every hour that we were not in bed, or at school, was spent in setting type or pulling the press. It was not uncommon for Ned to work with a sandwich on the corner of his case ; and, as often as he came to a period, he would stop and take a bite.

"This is the way Barnum used to do," said he, " when he started his museum—take his lunch with him, and stay right there. It 's the only way to make a great American success "—and he took another bite, his dental semicircle this time inclosing a portion of the bread that bore a fine proof-impression of his thumb and finger in printer's ink.

Though Phaeton was not able, for some time, to take a hand at the work, he rendered good service by directing things, as the head of the firm. He was often suspicious, where Ned and I would have been taken in at once, as to the circuses and minstrel shows for which the boys used to come and order tickets and programmes by the hundred, always proposing to pay for them out of the receipts of the show. The number of these had increased enormously, and it looked as if the boys got them up mainly for the sake of seeing themselves in print. Sometimes they would write out the most elaborate programmes, and then want them printed at once, before their enterprises had any existence except on paper. One boy, whose father was an actor, made out a complete cast of the play of " Romeo and Juliet," with himself for the part of *Romeo*, and Monkey Roe as *Juliet*.

One day a little curly-headed fellow, named Moses Green, came to the office, and wanted us to print a hundred tickets like this :

MOSE GREEN'S

MINSTREL SHOW.

Admit the Bearer.

" Where 's your show going to be ? " said Phaeton.

" I don't know," said Moses. " If Uncle James should sell his horses, perhaps he would let me have it in his barn."

" Yes, that would be a good place," said Phaeton. " And who are your actors ? "

" I don't know," said Moses. " But I 'm going to

ask Charlie Garrison, because he's got a good fife ; and
Lem Whitney, because he knows how to black up with
burnt cork ; and Andy Wilson, because he knows 'O
Susanna' all by heart."

"And what is the price of admission ? " said Phaeton.

"I don't know," said Moses. "But I thought if the
boys would n't pay five cents, I 'd take four."

"I 'll tell you what 't is, Moses," said Phaeton ; "we 're
badly crowded with work just now, and it would ac-
commodate us if you could wait a little while. Suppose
you engage your actors first, and rehearse the pieces that
you 're going to play, and get the barn rigged up, and
burn the cork, and make up your mind about the price ;
and then give us a call, and we 'll be happy to print your
tickets for you."

"All right," said Moses. "I 'll go home and burn a
cork, right away."

And he went off, whistling " O Susanna."

"Fay, I think that 's bad policy " said Ned, when
Moses was out of sight.

"I don't see how you can say that," said Phaeton.

"It 's as plain as day," said Ned. "We ought to
have gone right on and printed his tickets. Suppose he
has n't any show, and never will have one—what of it ?
We should n't suffer. His father would see that our bill
was paid. I 've heard Father say that Mr. Green was the
very soul of honor."

than honest," said Phaeton.

From the fact that our school has hardly been mentioned in this story, it must not be inferred that we were not all this time acquiring education by the usual methods. The performances here recorded took place out of school-hours, or on Saturdays, when there was no school. The events inside the temple of learning were generally so dull that they would hardly interest the story-reader.

Yet there was now and then an accident or exploit which relieved the tediousness of study-time. On one occasion, Robert Fox brought to school, as part of his luncheon, a bottle of pop-beer. An hour before intermission we were startled by a tremendous hissing and foaming sound, and the heads of the whole school were instantly turned toward the quarter whence it came. There was Fox with the palm of his hand upon the cork, which was half-way in the bottle that stood upon the floor beside his desk. Though he threw his whole weight upon it, he could not force it in any farther, and the beer rose like a fountain almost to the ceiling, and fell in a beautiful circle, of which Fox and his bottle were the interesting centre.

Any boy who has ever attended a school taught by an irascible master will readily imagine the sequel. Isaac Holman recorded the affair in the form of a Latin fable, which was so popular that we printed it. Here it is :

"IT ROSE LIKE A FOUNTAIN."

VULPES ET BEER.

Quondam vulpes bottulum poppi beeris in schola tulit, quod in arca reponebat. Sed corda laxa, ob vim beeris, cortex collum reliquit, et beer, spumans, se pavimento effudit. Deinde magister capit unum extremum lori, et vulpes alterum sentiebat. Hæc fabula docet that, when you bring pop-beer to school, you should tie the string so tight that it can't pop off before lunch-time.

When Jack-in-the-Box saw this fable, he said it was a good fable, and he was proud of his pupil, though some of the tenses were a little out of joint.

Holman said the reason why he put the moral in English was, because that was the important part of it, and ought to be in a language that everybody could understand.

Monkey Roe said he was glad to hear this explanation, as he had been afraid it was because Holman had got to the end of his Latin.

Charlie Garrison, in attempting to criticise the title of the fable, only exposed himself to ridicule.

"It must be a mistake," said he; "for you know you can't eat beer. It's plain enough that it ought to be, *Vulpes*" (he pronounced this word in one syllable) "*drank beer.*"

This shows the perils of ignorance. If Charlie had

had a thorough classical training, he would n't have made
such a mistake.   It was a curious fact that the boys who
had never studied Latin, and to whom the blunder had to
be explained, laughed at him more unmercifully than anybody else.

But Holman's literary masterpiece (if it was his) was
in rhyme, and in some respects it remains a mystery to
this day.

One evening he called to see me, and intimated that
he had some confidential business on hand, for which we
would better adjourn to the printing-office, and accordingly we went there.

" I want a job of printing done," said he, " provided
it can be done in the right way."

" We shall be glad to do it as well as we possibly
can," said I.   " What is it ? "

" I can't tell you what it is," said he.

" Well, let me see the manuscript," said I.

" There is n't any manuscript," said he.

" Oh, it is n't prepared yet ? " said I.   " When will
it be ready ? "

" There never will be any manuscript for it," said he.

I began to be puzzled.   Still, I remembered that small
signs and labels were often printed, consisting of only a
word or two, which did not require any copy.

" Is it a sign ? " said I.

" No."

" Labels ? "

" No."

" Then what in the world is it ? And how do you suppose I am going to print for you, unless I know what to print ? "

" That 's the point of the whole business," said Isaac. " I want you to let me come into your office, and use your type and press to print a little thing that concerns nobody but myself, and I don't care to have even you know about it. I want you to let me do all the work my-self, when you are not here, and I shall wash up the rollers, distribute the type, destroy all my proofs, and leave everything in the office as I found it. Of course I shall pay you the same as if you did the work."

" But how can you set the type ? " said I. " You don't even know the case, do you ? "

" No," said he ; " but I suppose the letters are all in it somewhere, and I can find them with a little searching."

" And do you know how to lock up a form ? " said I.

" I 've often seen you do it," said he ; " and I think I 'm mechanic enough to manage it."

" When do you want to go to work ? "

" *Duo eques, rectus ab* — to-night, right away."

" Very well — good night ! " said I.

When I went to the office next day, I found Ned busily at work trying to fit together some small torn scraps of pa-per. They were printed on one side, and, as fast as he found where one belonged, he fastened it in place by pasting it to a blank sheet which he had laid down as a foundation. When I arrived, the work had progressed as far as this:

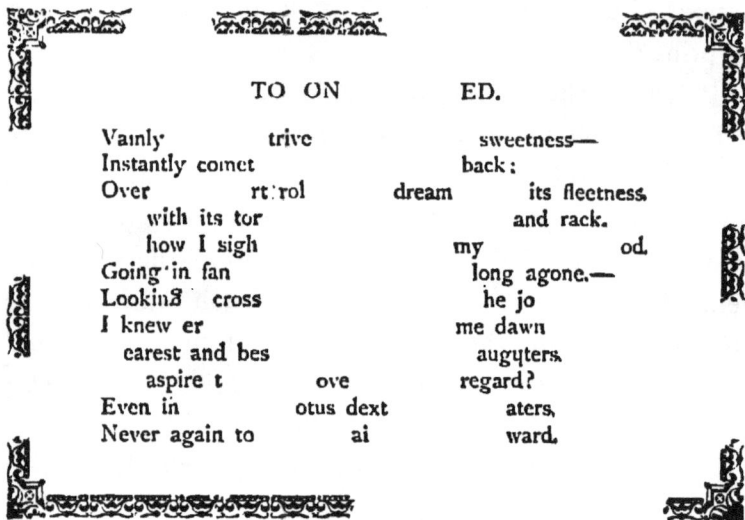

TO ON   ED.

Vainly	trive	sweetness—
Instantly comet		back:
Over	rt:rol	dream	its fleetness.
with its tor		and rack.
how I sigh		my	od.
Going in fan		long agone.—
Looking cross		he jo
I knew er		me dawn
earest and bes		augyters.
aspire t	ove	regard?
Even in	otus dext	aters.
Never again to	ai	ward.

" Here's a mystery," said Ned.

" What is it ? " said I.

" Did you print this ? " said he, suddenly looking into my face suspiciously.

" No," said I, calmly ; " I never saw it before."

" Well, then, somebody must have broken into our office last night.   For when I came in this morning, I found the oil all burned out of the big lamp,—I filled it yesterday, —and these torn scraps in the wood-box.   I got so many together pretty easily, but I can't find another one that will fit."

" It looks as if it had been a poem," said I.

"Yes," said Ned; "of course it was. And oh, look here! It was an acrostic, too!"

Ned took out his pencil, and filled in what he supposed to be the missing initial letters, making the name VIOLA GLIDDEN.

'It *may* have been an acrostic," said I; "but you can't tell with certainty, so much is missing."

"There is n't any doubt in my mind," said Ned; "and it's perfectly evident who was the burglar. Everybody knows who's sweet on Viola Glidden."

"I should think a good many would be sweet on her," said I; "she's the handsomest girl in town."

"Well, then," said Ned, "look at that ' otus dext.' Of course it was *totus dexter*,—and who's the boy that uses that classic expression? I would n't have thought that so nice a fellow as Holman would break in here at midnight, and put his mushy love-poetry into print at our expense. He must have been here about all night, for that lamp full of oil lasts nine hours."

"There's an easy way to punish him, whoever he was," said Phaeton, who had come in in time to hear most of our conversation.

"How is that?" said Ned.

"Get out a handbill," said Phaeton, "and spread it all over town, offering a reward of one cent for the conviction of the burglar who broke into our office last night and printed an acrostic, of which the following is a fac-simile of a mutilated proof. Then set up this, just as you have it here."

"That's it; that'll make him hop," said Ned. "I'll go to work on it at once."

"But," said I, "it'll make Miss Glidden hop too."

"Let her hop."

"But then perhaps her brother John will call around and make you hop."

"He can't do it," said Ned. "The man that owns a printing-press can make everybody else hop, and nobody can make him hop—unless it is a man that owns another press. Whoever tries to fight a printing-press always gets the worst of it. Father says so, and he knows, for he tried it on the *Vindicator* when he was running for sheriff and they slandered him."

At this point I explained that Holman had not come there without permission, and that he expected to pay for everything.

"Then why did n't you tell us that before?" said Phaeton.

"I was going to tell you he had been here," said I, "and that he did not want any of us to know what he printed. But when I saw that you had found that out, I thought perhaps, in fairness to him, I ought not to tell you *who* it was."

"All right," said Ned. "Of course, it's none of our business how much love-poetry Holman makes, or how spooney it is, or what girl he sends it to, if he pays for it all. But don't forget to charge him for the oil. By the way, so many of the boys owe us for printing, I've bought a blank-book to put the accounts in, or we shall forget some of them. Monkey Roe's mother paid for the 'Orphan Boy' yesterday. I'll put that down now. Half a dollar wasn't enough to charge her; we must make it up on the next job we do for her or Monkey."

While he was saying this, he wrote in his book:

Mrs. Roe per Monkey 12 *orphan boys* 50 *Paid.*

Hardly had he finished the entry, when the door of the office was suddenly opened, and Patsy Rafferty thrust in his head and shouted :

" Jimmy the Rhymer's killed ! "

" What ? "

" What ? "

" I say Jimmy the Rhymer's killed ! And you done it, too ! "

I am sorry that Patsy said " done," when he meant *did*. But he was a good-hearted boy, nevertheless ; and probably his excitement was what made him forget his grammar.

" What do you mean ? " said Ned, who had turned as pale as ashes.

" You ought to know what I mean," said Patsy. " Just because he had the bad luck to spill a few of your old types, you abused him like a pickpocket, and said

8

he'd got to pay for 'em, and drove him out of the office. And he's been down around the depot every day since, selling papers, tryin' to make money enough to pay you. And now he's got runned over be a hack, when he was goin' across the street to a gentleman that wanted a paper. And they've took him home, — and his blood's all along the road, — and my mother says it's on your head, too, you miserable skinflint! I won't have any of your gifts!"

And with that Patsy thrust his hand into his pocket, drew out the visiting-cards that Ned had printed for him, and threw them high into the room, so that in falling they scattered over everything.

"I'll bring back your car," he continued, "as soon as I can get it. I lent it to Teddy Dwyer last week."

Then he shut the door with a bang, and went away.

We looked at one another in consternation.

"What shall we do?" said Ned.

"I think we ought to go to Jimmy's house at once," said I.

"Yes, of course," said Ned.

And he and I started. Phaeton went the other way— as we afterward learned, to inform his mother, who had long been noted for her benevolence in cases of distress and sorrow among her neighbors.

Ned and I not only went by the postern, but made a bee-line for Jimmy's house, going over any number of fences, and straight through door-yards, grass-plots, and garden-patches, without the slightest reference to streets or paths.

We left in such a hurry that we forgot to lock up the office. While we were gone, Monkey Roe sauntered in, found Holman's acrostic which Ned had pieced together, and, when he went away, carried it with him.

CHAPTER XIII.

A LYRIC STRAIN.

THE impulse which had sent Ned and me headlong toward Jimmy's home as soon as we heard of the accident, found itself exhausted when we reached the gate. As if by concert, we both came to a dead halt.

"What shall we do?" said Ned. "If Jimmy was alive, we could whistle and call him out; or we might even go and knock at the door. But I don't know how to go into a house where somebody's dead. I wish we had gone first and asked Jack-in-the-Box what was the right way to do."

"Perhaps Jimmy is n't dead," said I. "There 's no black crape on the door."

"That does n't prove it," said Ned; "for Jimmy's folks might not have any crape in the house."

While we were still debating the question, the front door opened, and Jack-in-the-Box came out.

"You 're the very boy — I mean man — I wanted to see," said Ned, running up to him, and speaking in a whisper.

"That 's fortunate," said Jack. "Tell me what I can do for you."

"Why, you see," said Ned, "we came right over here as soon as we heard about Jimmy. But we don't know the right way to go into a house where anybody's dead. We never did it before."

"Jimmy is n't dead," said Jack.

Ned literally gave a great bound. I suppose he felt as if he had been suddenly acquitted of a serious charge of murder.

"Oh, Jack, how lovely!" said he, and threw his arms around Jack's neck. "But I suppose he must be hurt, though?"

"Yes," said Jack, "he's pretty badly hurt."

"Still, if he's alive, we can do something for him," said Ned.

"Oh, certainly!" said Jack. "A great deal can be done for him—a great deal has been done already. But I think you 'd better not go in to see him just yet. Wait a few days, till he gets stronger," and Jack hurried away.

We still lingered before the house, and presently a little girl came out, eyed us curiously, and then went to swinging on the chain that supported the weight which kept the gate shut.

"You don't seem to go along," said she, after a while.

We made no answer.

"Did you want to know about my brother Jimmy?" said she, after another pause.

"Yes," said I, " we'd be glad to hear all about him."

"Well, I'll tell you all about it," said she. "Jimmy's hurt very bad—because he was runned over by a wagon —because he got in the way—because he did n't see it— because a gentleman wanted a paper on the other side of the street—because Jimmy was selling them—because he wanted to get money—because he had to pay a great lot of it to a naughty, ugly boy that lives over that way somewhere—because he just touched one of that boy's old things, and it fell right to pieces. And he said Jimmy'd got to pay money for it, and should n't come in his house any more. And Jimmy was saving all his money to pay; and he's got two dollars and a half already from the papers, besides a dollar that Isaac Holman gave him to write a poem for him. And that makes almost five dollars, I guess."

"Let's go home," said Ned.

But I lingered to ask one question of the voluble little maiden.

"What poem did Jimmy write for Isaac Holman?"

"I don't know," she answered. "It's the only poem Jimmy ever would n't read to me. He said it was very particular, and he must n't let anybody see it."

A literary light dawned in upon me, as we slowly walked away.

Ned was silent for a long time. At last he spoke.

"I feel sick," said he.

" What 's the matter ? " said I.

" The matter is," said he, " that everybody seems to be trying to make out that it 's all my fault that Jimmy got hurt."

" Patsy Rafferty and Jimmy's sister are not everybody," said I.

" Of course not ; but they only talk what they hear other people say."

" I suppose you were a little to blame," said I.

" Perhaps I was," said Ned, " and I wish I could do something for him. I 'd get any amount of money out of Aunt Mercy — if money would do him any good."

As our way home led us past Jack's box, I suggested that we should stop and consult him about it.

" Jack," said Ned, " please tell us exactly how it is about Jimmy."

" The poor boy is fearfully hurt," said Jack. " One leg is broken, and the other badly bruised."

" Do you know of anything we can do for him ? "

" What do you think of doing ? " said Jack.

" If money was wanted," said Ned, and the tears started in his eyes, " I could work on Aunt Mercy's feelings and get him any amount."

Jack drummed with his fingers on the arm of his chair, and said nothing for some minutes. Then he spoke slowly.

" I doubt if the family would accept a gift of money from any source."

"Could n't I, at least, pay the doctor's bill ? " said Ned.

"You might," said Jack.

"Yes, of course," said Ned ; "I can go to the doctor privately, and tell him not to charge them a cent, and Aunt Mercy 'll pay him. That 's the way to do it. What doctor do they have ? "

"Dr. Grill."

"Dr. Grill ! " Ned repeated in astonishment. "Why, Dr. Grill does n't know anything at all. Father says somebody said if a sick man was made of glass, and had a Drummond light in his stomach, Dr. Grill could n't see what ailed him."

"We don't need a Drummond light to see what ails Jimmy," said Jack, quietly.

"Still," said Ned, "he ought to have a good doctor. Can't you tell them to get Dr. Campbell ? Father says he has tied the croaking artery nineteen times. Dr. Campbell is the man for my money ! But how queer it must feel to have nineteen hard knots tied in your croaking artery. Do you think Jimmy's croaking artery will have to be tied up, Jack ? If it does, I tell you what, Dr. Campbell 's the man to do it."

Jack laughed immoderately. But Ned was not the only person who ever made himself ridiculous by recommending a physician too enthusiastically.

"I don't see what you 're laughing at," said he. "It seems to me it 's a pretty serious business."

" I was only laughing at a harmless little mistake of yours," said Jack. " When you said 'the croaking artery,' I presume you meant the carotid artery — this one here in the side of the neck."

" If that 's the right name of it, that 's what I meant," said Ned.

" And when your father said Dr. Campbell had tied it nineteen times," continued Jack, " he did n't mean that he had tied nineteen hard knots in one person's, but that he had had occasion to tie the artery in nineteen different persons."

" And will Jimmy's have to be tied ? " said Ned.

" As the carotid artery is in the neck, and Jimmy's injuries are all in his legs, I should say not," said Jack.

" Of course not ; I might have thought of that," said Ned. " But you see, Jack, I don't know much about doctor-things anyway, and to-day I don't know what I do know, for everybody 's been saying I 'm to blame for Jimmy's hurt, and making me feel like a murderer. I 'll do whatever you say, Jack. If you say run for Dr. Campbell, I 'll go right away."

" I think Dr. Grill will do everything that ought to be done," said Jack. " There 's nothing you can do now, but perhaps we can think of something when Jimmy begins to get well."

" Then you think he will get well ? " said Ned.

" I hope he will," said Jack.

S*

" I tell you what 't is," said Ned, as we continued our walk toward home, " that Jack-in-the-Box is the nicest fellow that ever waved a flag. Sometimes I think he knows more than Father does."

A day or two later, Ned went to see his aunt, and I went with him.

" Aunt Mercy," said he, " one of the best boys in this town has got badly hurt — run over down by the depot — and his folks are so awful poor I don't see what they 're going to do."

" Yes, I heard about it," said Aunt Mercy. " It was that wretched, brutal brother of yours who was to blame for it all."

" Oh no, Aunty, Fay had nothing at all to do with it," said Ned.

" Don't tell me, child ; you need n't try to shield your wicked brother ; I know all about it. Miss Pinkham came to call on me, and told me the whole story. She said the poor little fellow tipped over a type or something, and one of those Rogers boys drove him away, and swore at him dreadfully, and made him go and sell papers under the wheels of the cars and omnibuses, to get money to pay for it. Of course I knew which one it was, but I did not say anything, I felt so deeply mortified for the family."

It is difficult to say what answer Ned ought to have made to this. To convince his aunt that Miss Pinkham's version of the story was incorrect, would have been hopeless; to plead guilty to the indictment as it stood, would have been unjust to himself; and to leave matters as they were, seemed unjust to his brother. And above all was the consideration that if he vexed his aunt, he would probably defeat the whole object of his visit — getting help for Jimmy. So he remained silent.

"What were you going to say, Edmund Burton, about poor Jimmy Redmond?" said his aunt.

"I was going to say," Ned answered, "that I wished I could help him a little by paying his doctor's bill, and not let him know anything about it."

"You lovely, benevolent boy!" exclaimed Aunt Mercy, "that's exactly what you shall do. You're an ornament to the family. Your right hand does n't know what your left hand's doing. As soon as you find out what the doctor's bill is, come to me, and I'll furnish you the money. Oh, what a pity that hard-hearted brother wont follow your noble example."

Jimmy had the best of care; Mrs. Rogers did a great deal, in a quiet, almost unnoticeable way, to add to his comforts; and after a while it was announced that he might receive short visits from the boys.

Phaeton, Ned, and I were his first visitors. We found him lying in a little room where the sunbeams poured in at a south window, but not till they had been broken into all sorts of shapes by the foliage of a wistaria, the shadows of which moved with every breeze to and fro across a breadth of rag carpet.

The walls were ornamented with a dozen or twenty pictures—some of them out of old books and papers, and some drawn and painted in water-colors by Jimmy himself—none of them framed. The water-colors were mainly illustrations of his own poems. I am not able to say whether they possessed artistic merit, for I was a boy at the time, and of course a boy, who only knows what pleases him, can not be expected to know what is artistic and ought to please him. But some of them appeared to me very wonderful, especially one that illustrated "The Unlucky Fishermen." It was at the point where Joe and Isaac were trying to catch a ride behind an omnibus. Not only did the heroes themselves appear completely tired out by the long day of fruitless fishing, but the dog looked tired, the bus horses were evidently tired, the driver was tired, the boy who called out "Whip behind!" was tired, even the bus itself had a tired look, and this general air of weariness produced in the picture a wonderful unity of effect.

Jimmy looked so pale and thin, as he lay there, that we were all startled, and Ned seemed actually frightened. He lost control of himself, and broke out passionately:

"Oh, Jimmy, dear Jimmy, you must n't die! We can't have you die! We 'll get all the doctors in the city, and buy you everything you need, only don't die!"

"JIMMY LOOKED SO PALE AND THIN, AS HE LAY THERE."

Here he thrust his hand into his pocket, and brought out two silver dollars.

"Take them, Jimmy, take them!" said he. "Aunt Mercy's got plenty more that you can have when these are gone. And we don't care anything about the type you pied. I'd rather pi half the type in the office than see your leg broken. We can't any of us spare you. Live, Jimmy, live! and you may be proof-reader in our office,—we need one dreadfully, Jack-in-the-Box says so, —and you know pretty nearly everything, and can soon learn the rest, and we'll get you the green shade for your eyes, and you're awful round-sho—that is, I mean, in fact, I think you are the very man for it. And you can grow up with the business, and always have a good place. And then, Jimmy, if you want to use your spare time in setting up your poems, you may, and change them just as much as you want to, and we won't charge you a cent for the use of the type."

Ned certainly meant this for a generous offer, and Jimmy seemed to consider it so; but if he could have taken counsel of some of the sad-faced men who have spent their lives in proof-reading, I think, perhaps, he would have preferred to die.

Ned had scarcely finished his apostrophe, when Jimmy's little sister brought in a beautiful bouquet, sent by Miss Glidden to brighten up the sick boy's chamber.

Looking around, we saw that other friends had been

equally thoughtful. Isaac Holman had sent a basket of fruit; Monkey Roe, a comic almanac, three or four years old, but just as funny; Jack-in-the-Box a bottle of cordial; and Patsy Rafferty, a small bag of marbles. Whether these last had been acquired by honest purchase, or by the gambling operation known as " playing for good," it would be ungenerous to inquire.

" How do you amuse yourself, Jimmy ? " said Phaeton.

" I don't have much amusement," answered Jimmy; " but still I can write a little."

" Poetry ? " said Phaeton.

" Oh, yes," said Jimmy; " I write very little except poetry. There 's plenty of prose in the world already."

" Perhaps," said Phaeton, " if you feel strong enough, you 'll read us your latest poem."

" Yes, certainly, if you 'd like to hear it," said Jimmy. " Please pull out a box that you 'll see under the head of my bed here."

Phaeton thrust his arm under, and pulled out a pine box, which was fastened with a small brass padlock.

" The key is under the dying hound," said Jimmy.

Looking around the room, we saw that one of Jimmy's pictures represented a large dog dying, and a little boy and girl weeping over it. Whether it was Beth Gelert, or some other heroic brute, I do not know. The corner of this picture being lifted, disclosed a small key, hung over the head of a carpet-tack driven into the wall.

When the box was opened, we saw that it was nearly full of manuscripts.

"The last one," said Jimmy, who could not turn from his one position on the bed, "is written on blue paper, with a piece torn off from the upper right-hand corner."

Phaeton soon found it, and handed it to Jimmy.

"It is called an 'Ode to a Horseshoe'—that one over the door," said Jimmy. "I found it in the road the day before I was hurt, and brought it right home, and put it up there."

"Then it has n't brought you much good luck, so far, has it?" said Phaeton.

"I don't know about that," said Jimmy. "It's true I was hurt the very next day; but something seems to have brought me a great many good friends."

"Oh! you always had those, horseshoe or no horse-shoe," said Ned.

"I 'm glad if I did," said Jimmy; "though I never suspected it. But now I should like to read you the poem, and get your opinions on it; because it's in a different vein from most of my others." And then Jimmy read us his verses :

ODE TO A HORSESHOE.

Thou relic of departed horse !
  Thou harbinger of luck to man !
When things seem growing worse and worse,
  How good to find thee in the van !

A hundred thousand miles, I ween !
   You 've travelled on the flying heel —
By country roads, where fields were green,
   O'er pavements, with the rattling wheel.

Your toe-calk, in that elder day,
   Was sharper than a serpent's tooth ;
But now it 's almost worn away ;
   The blacksmith should renew its youth.

Bright is the side was next the ground,
   And dark the side was next the hoof ;
'T is thus true metal 's only found
   Where hard knocks put it to the proof.

For aught I know, you may have done
   Your mile in two nineteen or twenty ;
Or, on a dray-horse, never run,
   But walked and walked, and pulled a plenty.

At last your journeys all are o'er,
   Whether of labor or of pleasure,
And there you hang above my door,
   To bring me health and strength and treasure.

When the reading was finished we all remained silent, till Jimmy spoke.

"I should like to have you give me your opinions about it," said he. "Don't be afraid to criticise it. Of course, there must be faults in it."

"That 's an awful good moral about the hard knocks," said I.

"Yes," said Phaeton, "it might be drawn from Jimmy's own experience. And as he says, the poem does seem to be in a new vein. I noticed a good many words that were different from any in his other pieces."

"That," said Jimmy, "is because I've been studying some of the older poets lately. Jack-in-the-Box lent me Shakespeare, and I got three or four others from the school library. Probably they have had some effect on my style."

Ned walked to the door, and, standing tiptoe, looked intently at the horseshoe.

"One thing is certain," said he, "that passage about the toe-calk is perfectly true to nature. The toe-calk is nearly worn away, and the heel-calks are almost as bad."

".It's a good poem," said I. "I don't see how you could make it any better."

"Nor I," said Phaeton. "It tells the whole story."

"I'm glad you like it," said Jimmy. "I felt a little uncertain about dipping into the lyric strain."

"Yes," said Ned; "there's just one spot where it shows the strain, and I don't see another thing wrong about it."

"What's that?" said Jimmy.

"Perhaps we'd better not talk about it till you get well," said Ned.

"Oh, never mind that," said Jimmy. "I don't need my legs to write poetry with, or to criticise it, either."

"Well," said Ned, "I hate to find fault with it, because it's such a good poem, and I enjoyed it so much; but it seems to me you've strained the truth a little where you say 'a hundred thousand miles.'"

" How so ?" said Jimmy.

" Calculate it for yourself," said Ned. " No horse is likely to travel more than about fifty miles a day. And if he did that every day, he'd go three hundred miles in a week. At that rate, it would take him more than six years to travel a hundred thousand miles. But no shoe lasts a horse six years—nor one year, even. So, you see, this could n't have travelled a hundred thousand miles. That's why I say the lyric strain is strained a little too much."

"I see," said Jimmy. " You are undoubtedly right. I shall have to soften it down to a dozen thousand, or something like that."

" Yes," said Ned; " soften it down. When that's done, the poem will be perfect; there wont be a single fact misstated in it."

At this point, Phaeton said he thought we had staid as long as we ought to, and should be going.

" I wish, Jimmy," said Ned, " you'd let me take this poem and read it to Jack-in-the-Box. I know he would enjoy it."

"I've no objection," said Jimmy. " And if you can find time some day to print it for me, here's two dollars to pay for the job," and he thrust Ned's money back into his hand.

"All right!" said Ned, as he saw that Jimmy would
not accept the money, and yet did not want to refuse it
rudely. "We 'll try to make a handsome job of it. Perhaps some day it will be printed on white satin, and hung
up in the Emperor of China's palace, like—whose poem
was it Father told about the other day, Fay ? "

"Derzhavin's," said Phaeton.

"Yes, Derzhavin's, whoever he was," said Ned.
"And this one of Jimmy's ought to have a horseshoe
embroidered in gold thread on the corner of the satin.
But those funny ladies with slant eyes and little club feet
will have to do that. I suppose they have n't much else
to keep them busy, as they 're not able to do any house-
work. It might have a small gold horseshoe on each of
the four corners, or it might have one big horseshoe sur-
rounding the poem. Which do you think you would like
best, Jimmy ? "

"I 've no choice ; either would suit me," answered
the poet.

"Good-bye, Jimmy ! "

"Good-bye, boys ! "

CHAPTER XIV.

AN ALARM OF FIRE.

EVERY day some one of us called to see Jimmy. He was well taken care of, and got along nicely. Jack-in-the-Box lent him books, and each day a fresh bouquet was sent in by Miss Glidden.

One day Monkey Roe called on him.

"Jimmy," said he, "you know all about poetry, I suppose."

"I know something about it," said Jimmy. "I have written considerable."

"And are you well enough yet to undertake an odd job in it?"

"Oh, yes," said Jimmy. "A fellow does n't have to be very well to write poetry."

"It is n't exactly writing poetry that I want done," said Monkey. "It's a very odd job, indeed. You might call it repairing poetry. Do poets ever repair poetry, as well as make it new?"

"I don't know," said Jimmy. "I should think it might be done in some cases."

"Well, now," said Monkey, "I have a broken poem.

Some part of every line is gone. But the rhymes are all there, and many of the other words, and most of the beginnings of the lines. I thought a poet would know how to fill up all the blank spaces, and make it just as it was when it was whole."

"I don't know," said Jimmy, doubtfully. "It might be possible to do it, and it might not. I'll do what I can for you. Let me see it, if you have it with you."

Monkey pulled out of his pocket the mutilated poem of Holman's which Ned had pieced together, and, after smoothing it out, handed it to Jimmy.

As Jimmy looked it over, he turned every color which it is possible for an unhappy human countenance to assume, and then gave a heavy groan.

"Where did you get this, Monkey?" said he.

"Found it," said Monkey.

"Found it — impossible!" said Jimmy.

"Upon my word, I did find it, and just in the shape you see it now. But what of it?"

"Where did you find it?" said Jimmy.

"In Rogers's printing-office, kicking around on the floor. It seemed to be thrown away as waste paper; so I thought there was no harm in taking it. And when I read it, it looked to me like a curious sort of puzzle, which I thought would interest you. But you seem to take it very seriously."

"It's a serious matter," said Jimmy.

" No harm done, I hope," said Monkey.

" There may be," said Jimmy. " I can't tell. Some things about it I can't understand. I must ask you to let me keep this."

" If it 's so very important," said Monkey, " it ought to be taken back to Phaeton Rogers, as it was in his office that I found it."

" No," said Jimmy ; " it does n't belong to him."

" Then you know something about it ? " said Monkey.

" Yes, Monkey," said Jimmy, " I do know considerable about it. But it is a confidential matter entirely, and I shall have to insist on keeping this."

" All right ! " said Monkey. " I 'll take your word for it."

A few days after this, we were visiting Jack in his box, when, as he was turning over the leaves of his scrapbook to find something he wanted to show us, Phaeton exclaimed :

" What 's that I saw ? " and, turning back a leaf or two, pointed to an exact fac-simile of the mutilated poem. It had evidently been made by laying a sheet of oiled paper over the original, and carefully tracing the letters with a pencil.

" Oh, that," said Jack, " is something that Monkey Roe brought here. He said it was a literary puzzle, and wanted me to see if I could restore the lines. I 've been so busy I have n't tried it yet."

Phaeton at once wrote a note to Monkey, asking him to bring back the original; whereupon Monkey called at the office and explained why he could not return it.

"All right! I'll see Jimmy about it myself," said Phaeton. " But have you made any other tracings of it besides the one Jack-in-the-Box has ? "

" Only two others," said Monkey.

" Where are they ? "

" One I have at home."

" And the other ? "

" I sent it to Miss Glidden, with a note saying that, as I had heard she wrote poetry sometimes, I thought she might be interested in this poetical puzzle."

" Good gracious ! " said Phaeton. " There's no use in trying to dip up *that* spilled milk."

In those days there was an excitement and pleasure enjoyed by many boys, which was denied to Phaeton, Ned, and me. This was the privilege of running to fires. Nearly all large fires occurred in the night, and Mr. Rogers would not permit his boys to turn out from their warm beds and run at breathless speed to the other side of the town to see a building burned. So they had to lie still and possess their souls in impatience while they heard the clanging of the bells and the rattling of the engine, and perhaps saw through their window the lurid reflection on the midnight sky. There was no need for

9

my parents to forbid me, since none of these things ever woke me.

Running to fires, at least in cities, is now a thing of the past. The alarm is communicated silently by telegraph to the various engine-houses, a team is instantly harnessed to the engine, and with two or three men it is driven to the fire, which is often extinguished without the inhabitants of the next street knowing that there has been a fire at all.

At the time of this story, the steam fire-engine had not been invented, and there were no paid fire departments. The hand-engine had a long pole on each side, called a brake, fastened to a frame that worked up and down like a pump-handle. When the brake on one side was down, that on the other was up. The brakes were long enough for nearly twenty men to stand in a row on each side and work them. No horses were used, but there was a long double rope, called a drag-rope, by which the men themselves drew the engine from its house to the fire. They always ran at full speed, and the two men who held the tongue, like the tongue of a wagon, had to be almost as strong as horses, to control and guide it as it went bumping over the pavement.

Each engine had a number and a name, and there was an organized company, of from forty to seventy men, who had it in charge, managed it at fires, drew it out on parade-days, took pride in it, and bragged about it.

The partiality of the firemen for their own engine and company was as nothing in comparison with that of the boys. Every boy in town had a violent affection for some one company, to the exclusion of all others. It might be because his father or his cousin belonged to that company, or because he thought it had the handsomest uniform (for no two companies were uniformed alike), or because it was first on the ground when his uncle's store was on fire, or because he thought it was the company destined to "wash" all others. Sometimes there would be no discoverable reason for his choice; yet the boy would be just as strong in his partisanship, and often his highest ambition would be to be able to run with the hose-cart of his favorite company. The hose was carried wound on a reel, trundled on two light wheels, which was managed by half a dozen boys, fifteen or sixteen years of age.

. When a fire broke out, the bells of all the churches were rung; first slowly, striking one, two, three, four, etc., according to which district of the town the fire was in, and then clanging away with rapid strokes. Thus the whole town was alarmed, and a great many people besides the firemen ran to every fire. Firemen jumped from their beds at the first tap of a bell; or, if it was in the day-time, they instantly threw down their tools, left their work, and ran.

There was an intense rivalry as to which engine

should first get to the fire, and which should pour the most effective stream of water upon it. But the highest pitch of excitement was reached when there was an opportunity to " wash." If the fire was too far from the water-supply to be reached through the hose of a single engine, one engine would be stationed at the side of the river or canal, or wherever the water was taken from, to pump it up and send it as far as it could through its hose, there discharging into the box of another engine, which, in turn, forced it another distance, through its own hose. If the first engine could send the water along faster than the second could dispose of it, the result would be that in a few minutes the box of the second would be overflowed, and she was then said to be " washed," which was considered a great triumph for the company that had washed her.

This sort of rivalry caused the firemen to do their utmost, and they did not always confine themselves to fair means. Sometimes, when an engine was in danger of being washed, some member of the company would follow the line of the other company's hose till he came to where it passed through a dark place, and then, whipping out his pocket-knife, would cut it open and run away. When there were not enough members of a company present to man the brakes, or when they were tired out, the foreman had the right to select men from among the bystanders, and compel them to take hold.

Monkey Roe was a born fireman. He never failed to hear the first tap of the bell, about ninety seconds after which he dropped from the casement of his window to the roof of the kitchen, thence to the roof of the back piazza, slid down a pillar, and was off for the fire, generally following in the wake of Red Rover Three, which was the company he sided with. It was entertaining to hear him relate his exciting adventures; but it was also somewhat exasperating.

"I don't see," said Ned, after Monkey had finished one of these thrilling narratives, "what Father means by never letting us run to a fire. How does he suppose he 's going to make men of us, if we never begin to do anything manly?"

"Perhaps he does n't think it is especially manly," said Phaeton.

"Not manly!" exclaimed Ned, in astonishment. "I should like to know what 's more manly than to take the tongue of Big Six when there 's a tremendous fire and they jump her all the way down State street. Or to stand on the engine and yell at the men, when Torrent Two is trying to wash her. Why, sometimes the foreman gets so excited that he batters his trumpet all to pieces, pounding on the brakes, to cheer his men."

"Knocking trumpets to pieces is very manly, of course," said Phaeton, smiling. "I did n't mean to say Father would n't consider it manly to be a fireman.

What I should have said was, that perhaps he thought there were other ways to become manly. I should like to run to a fire once in a while ; not for the sake of manliness, but to see the fun."

The more Ned thought about it, the more it seemed to him it was a continuous wrong. At last he spoke to his father about it, and set forth so powerfully the danger of growing up without becoming manly, that Mr. Rogers laughingly told the boys they might run to the very next fire.

The next thing was to count me in. The only difficulty to be overcome in my case was sleepiness. We canvassed many plans. Ned suggested a pistol fastened to the side of my window, with a string tied to the trigger and reaching to the ground, so that he or Phaeton could pull it on their way to the fire. The serious objection to this was that a shower would prevent the pistol from going off. It was also suggested that I have a bell, or tie the cord to a chair or something that could be pulled over and make a racket.

" The objection to all those things is," said Phaeton, " that they will disturb the whole family. Now, if you would make a rope-ladder, and hang it out of your window every night, one of us could climb up quietly, and speak to you. Then you could get out at the window and come down the ladder, instead of going through the house and waking up the people."

This suggestion struck us with great force ; it doubled the anticipated romance. Under instructions from Phaeton, Ned and I made the ladder. In the store-room we found a bed-cord, which answered well for the sides. The rungs must be made of wood, and we had considerable difficulty in finding anything suitable. Any wood that we could have cut would be so soft that the rungs, to be strong enough, must have been very bulky. This was an objection, as I was to roll up the ladder in the day-time, and hide it under my bed. At last, Ned came over to tell me he had found just the thing, and took me to the attic of their house to see.

"There," said he, pointing to half a dozen ancient-looking chairs in a cobwebbed corner. "That is exactly what we want. The rounds of those old chairs are as tough as iron."

"Whose chairs are they ? " said I.

"Oh, anybody's, nobody's," said Ned. " I suppose they are a hundred years old. And who's ever going to sit in such awkward-looking old things as those ? "

It did seem preposterous to suppose that anybody would ; so we went to work to take out the rounds at once. The old chairs were very strong, and after we had pulled at them in vain to spring them apart enough for the rounds to drop out, we got a saw and sawed off all the rounds an inch or two from the legs.

With these, the ladder was soon made, and I went

home and drove two great spikes into the sill of my window, to hang it by.

I used to hang out the ladder every night, and take it in every morning. The first two nights I lay awake till almost daylight, momentarily expecting the stroke of the fire-bell. But it was not heard on those nights, nor the next, nor the next.

" It would be just like our luck," said Ned, " if there should never be another fire in this town."

" It would be lucky for the town," said Phaeton, who overheard him.

" Perhaps so," said Ned; " and yet I could point out some houses that would look a great deal better burned up. I wonder if it would do any good to hang a horse-shoe over the door."

" What for ? " said Phaeton. " To prevent them from burning ? "

" Oh, no," said Ned. " I mean over the door of our office, to — to — well, not exactly to make those houses burn, but to bring us good luck generally."

It did seem a long time for the town to be without a conflagration, and one day Ned came into the office looking quite dejected.

" What do you think has happened now ? " said he. " Just like our luck, only worse and worse."

" What is it ? " said I.

" The whole fire department 's going to smash."

"I should n't think you 'd call that bad luck," said Phaeton. "For now when there *is* a fire, it will be a big one, if there 's no fire department to prevent it from spreading."

"But the best fun," said Ned, "is to see the firemen handle the fire, and to see Red Rover Three wash Cataract Eight. I saw her do it beautifully at annual inspection. What I want is a tremendous big fire, and plenty of engines to play on it."

The explanation of Ned's alarming intelligence was that the fire department had got into a quarrel with the common council, and threatened to disband. One company, who had rather a shabby engine-house, and were refused an appropriation for a new one, tied black crape on the brakes of their engine, drew it through the principal streets, and finally, stopping before the court-house yard, lifted the machine bodily and threw it over the fence. Then they threw their fireman hats after it, and quietly disbanded. This company had been known as Reliance Five. The incident frightened the common council into giving the other companies what they asked for ; but there was never more a Number Five company in that city.

I had got pretty tired of hanging out my rope ladder every night, and rolling it up every morning, when at last the hour of destiny struck, as the majority of poets would say — that is, the court-house bell struck the third district, and steeple after steeple caught up the tune, till,

9*

in a few minutes, the whole air was full of the wild clangor of bells. At the same time, the throats of innumerable men and boys were open, and the word "Fire!" was pouring out from them in a continuous stream.

"Wake up, Ned!" said Phaeton. "Here it is at last, and it's a big one."

Ned bounded to his feet, looked out at the window, exclaimed "Oh, glory!" as he saw the lurid sky, and then began to get into his clothes with the utmost rapidity. Suddenly he stopped.

"Look here, Fay," said he. "This is Sunday night. I'm afraid Father wont let us go, after all."

"Perhaps not," said Phaeton.

"Then, what must we do?" said Ned.

"Do the best we can."

"The question is, what *is* best?" said Ned. "It is evident we ought to go out of the window, but it's too high from the ground."

"Then we must make a rope," said Phaeton.

"What can we make it of?"

"The bedclothes, of course."

"That's a splendid idea!—that saves us," said Ned, and he set about tying the sheets together.

Before Phaeton was dressed, Ned had made the rope and cast it out of the window, first tying one end to the bedpost, and sliding down to the ground, made off, without waiting for his brother.

"NED LOOKED UP INTO THE FACE OF A POLICEMAN."

He came straight to my ladder, and had his foot on the first rung, when a heavy hand was laid upon his shoulder.

"So you 're the one he sends in, are you?" said a deep voice, and Ned looked up into the face of a policeman. "I 'd rather have caught the old one," he continued, "but you 'll do. I 've been watching this burglar arrangement for two hours. And by the way, I must have some of it for evidence ; the old one may take it away while I 'm disposing of you." And he turned and with his pocket-knife cut off about a yard of my ladder, taking which in one hand and Ned in the other, he hurried away to the police-station.

It was useless for Ned to protest that he was not a burglar, nor a burglar's partner, or to tell the true story of the ladder, or to ask to be taken to his father. The policeman considered himself too wise for any such delusive tricks.

"Mr. Rogers's boy, eh?" said he. "Why don't you call yourself George Washington's boy, while you 're about it?"

"Washington never had any boys," said Ned.

"Did n't eh? Well, now, I congratulate George on that. A respectable man never knows what his sons may come to, in these times."

"Washington did n't live in these times," said Ned ; "he died hundreds of years ago."

"Did, eh?" said the policeman. "I see that you 're

a great scholard ; you can go above me in the history class, young man. I never was no scholard myself, but I know one when I see him ; and I always feel bad to put a scholard in quod."

"If I had my printing-office and a gun here," said Ned, "I 'd put plenty of quads into you."

"Would, eh ? " said the policeman. "Well, now, it 's lucky for me that that are printing-office and them ere quads are quietly reposing to-night in the dusky realms of imagination, aint it, young man ? But here 's the quod *I* spoke about — it 's reality, you see." And they ascended the steps of the station-house.

In the midst of sound sleep, I woke on hearing my name called, and saw the dark outlines of a human head and shoulders at my window, projected against a background of illuminated sky. I had heard Father reading an article in the evening paper about a gang of burglars being in the town, and I suppose that in my half-wakened condition that mingled itself vaguely in my thoughts with the idea of fire. At any rate, I seized a pitcher of water and threw its contents toward the light, and then, clubbing the pitcher, was about to make a desperate assault on the supposed burglar, when he spoke again.

"What are you doing ?   Don't you know me ? "

"Oh, is that you, Fay ? "

"Yes, and you 've drenched me through and through," said he, as he climbed in.

was about."

"It's a tremendous fire," said he, "and I hate to lose the time to go back home and change my clothes. Besides, I don't know that I could, for we made a rope of the bedclothes and slid down from our window, and I could n't climb up again."

"Oh, never mind, put on a suit of mine," said I, and got out my Sunday suit, the only clothes I had that seemed likely to be large enough for Phae-

PHAETON IS TAKEN FOR A BURGLAR.

ton. It was a tight squeeze, but he got into them.

"Why did you make your ladder so short?" said he.

"It reaches to the ground," said I.

" No, it does n't " said Phaeton ; " I had hard work to get started on it.   I expected to find Ned standing at the foot of it, but he was so impatient to see the fire, I suppose he could n't wait for us."

We dropped from the shortened ladder to the ground, passed out at the gate and shut it noiselessly behind us, and then broke into a run toward that quarter of the town where both a pillar of flame and a pillar of cloud rose through the night and lured us on.

At the same time our mouths opened themselves by instinct, and that thrilling word " Fire ! " was paid out continuously, like a sparkling ribbon, as we ran.

CHAPTER XV.

RUNNING WITH THE MACHINE.

PRESENTLY we heard a tremendous noise behind us,— a combination of rumble, rattle, and shout. It was Red Rover Three going to the fire. She was for some reason a little belated, and was trying to make up lost time. At least forty men had their hands on the drag-rope, and were taking her along at a lively rate, while the two who held the tongue and steered the engine, being obliged to run at the same time, had all they could do. The foreman was standing on the top, with a large tin trumpet in his hand, through which he occasionally shouted an order to the men.

" Let's take hold of the drag-rope and run with her," said Phaeton.

If I had been disposed to make any objection, I had no opportunity, for Phaeton immediately made a dive for a place where there was a longer interval than usual between the men, and seized the rope. Not to follow him would have seemed like desertion, and I thought if I was ever to be a boy of spirit, this was the time to begin.

When a boy for the first time laid his hand upon the

drag-rope of an engine under swift motion, he experienced a thrill of mingled joy and fear to which nothing else in boy-life is comparable. If he missed his hold, or tired too soon, he would almost certainly be thrown to the ground and run over. If he could hang on, and make his legs fly fast enough, he might consider himself as sharing in the glory when the machine rolled proudly up in the light of the burning building, and was welcomed with a shout.

There comes to most men, in early manhood, a single moment which perhaps equals this in its delicious blending of fear and rapture — but let us leave that to the poets.

Phaeton and I hung on with a good grip, while the inspiration of the fire in sight, and the enthusiasm of our company, seemed to lend us more than our usual strength and speed. But before we reached the fire, a noise was heard on a street that ran into ours at an angle some distance ahead. The foreman's ear caught it instantly, and he knew it was Cataract Eight doing her best in order to strike into the main road ahead of us.

"Jump her, men! jump her!" he shouted, and pounded on the brakes with his tin trumpet.

The eighty legs and four wheels on which Red Rover Three was making her way to the fire each doubled its speed, while forty mouths yelled "Ki yi!" and the excited foreman repeated his admonition to "Jump her, boys! jump her!"

"JUMP HER, BOYS! JUMP HER!"

Phaeton and I hung on for dear life, though I expected every moment to find myself unable to hang on any longer. Sometimes we measured the ground in a sort of seven-league-boot style, and again we seemed to be only as rags fastened to the rope and fluttering in the wind. The men at the tongue were tossed about in all sorts of ways. Sometimes one would be lying on his breast on the end of it where it curved up like a horse's neck, and the next minute one or both of them would be thrown almost under it. Whenever a wheel struck an uneven paving-stone, these men would be jerked violently to one side, and we could feel the shock all along the rope. It seemed sometimes as if the engine was simply being hurled through the air, occasionally swooping down enough in its flight to touch the ground and rebound again. All the while the church-bells of the city, in the hands of sextons doubly excited by fire and fees, kept up a direful clang. I doubt whether the celebrated clang of Apollo's silver bow could at all compare with it.

As we neared the forks of the road, the foreman yelled and pounded yet more vociferously, and through the din we could hear that Cataract Eight was doing the same thing. At last we shot by the corner just in time to compel our rival to fall in behind us, and a minute or two later we burst through the great ring of people that surrounded the fire, and made our entrance, as it were, upon the stage, with the roaring, crackling flames of three tall buildings for our mighty foot-lights.

We had jumped her.

The fire was in the Novelty Works — an establishment where were manufactured all sorts of small wares in wood and iron. The works occupied three buildings, pretty close together, surrounded by a small strip of yard. Either because the firemen, from the recent demoralization of the department, were long in coming upon the ground, or for some other reason, the fire was under good headway, and all three buildings were in flames, before a drop of water was thrown.

Phaeton whispered to me that we had better get away from the engine now, or they might expect us to work at the brakes; so we dodged back and forth through the crowd, and came out in front of the fire at another point. Here we met Monkey Roe, who had run with Red Rover's hose-cart, was flushed with excitement, and was evidently enjoying the fire most heartily.

"Oh, she's a big one!" said he, "probably the biggest we ever had in this town — or will be, before she gets through. I have great hopes of that old shanty across the road; it ought to have been burned down long ago. If this keeps on much longer, that 'll have to go. Don't you see the paint peeling off already?"

The "old shanty" referred to was a large wooden building used as a furniture factory, and it certainly did look as if Monkey's warmest hopes would be realized. I observed that he wore a broad belt of red leather, on which was inscribed the legend :

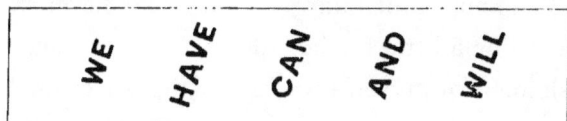

WE HAVE CAN AND WILL

" Monkey," said I, " what 's that ? "

" Why, don't you know that ? " said he ; " that 's Red Rover's motto."

" Yes, of course it is," said I ; " but what does it mean ? "

" It means," said Monkey, with solemn emphasis, " we have washed Eight, we can wash Eight, and we will wash Eight."

There were older people than Monkey Roe to whom the washing of Eight, rather than the extinguishing of fires, was the chief end of a company's existence.

" Yes," said I, catching some of Monkey's enthusiasm, in addition to what I had already acquired by running with Red Rover, " I think we can wash her."

The next moment I was pierced through and through by pangs of conscience. Here was I, a boy whose uncle was a member of Cataract Eight, and who ought, therefore, to have been a warm admirer and partisan of that company, not only running to a fire with her deadly rival, but openly expressing the opinion that she could be

washed.   But such is the force of circumstances in their
relative distance,— smaller ones that are near us often
counterbalancing much larger ones that happen, for the
moment, to be a little farther off.   It did not occur to me
to be ashamed of myself for expressing an opinion which
was not founded on a single fact of any kind whatever.
The consciences of very few people seem ever to be
troubled on that point.

"The Hook-and-Ladder is short-handed to-night,"
said Monkey.   "I think I'll take an axe."

"What does he mean by taking an axe?" said I to
Phaeton.

"I don't know," said Phaeton; "let's follow him,
and find out."

Monkey passed around the corner into the next street,
where stood a very long, light carriage, with two or three
ladders upon it and a few axes in sockets on the sides.
These axes differed from ordinary ones in having the corner of the head prolonged into a savage-looking spike.

Monkey spoke to the man in charge, who handed
him an axe and a fireman's hat.   This hat was made of
heavy sole-leather, painted black, the crown being
rounded into a hemisphere, and the rim extended behind
so that it covered his shoulder-blades.   On the front was
a shield ornamented with two crossed ladders, a trumpet,
and a large figure **2**.

He took the axe, and put on the hat, leaving his own,

and at the man's direction went to where a dozen axe-men were chopping at one side of a two-story wooden building that made a sort of connecting-link between the Novelty Works and the next large block.

Monkey seemed to hew away with the best of them ; and, though they were continually changing about, we could always tell him from the rest by his shorter stature and the fact that his hat seemed too large for him.

Before long, a dozen firemen, with a tall ladder on their shoulders, appeared from somewhere, and quickly raised it against the building. Three of them then mounted it, dragging up a pole with an enormous iron hook at the end. But there was no projection at the edge of the roof into which they could fix the hook.

"Stay where you are," shouted the foreman to them through his trumpet. Then to the assistant foreman he shouted :

"Send up your lightest man to cut a place."

The assistant foreman looked about him, seized on Monkey as the lightest man, and hastily ordered him up.

The next instant, Monkey was going up the ladder, axe in hand, passed the men who were holding the hook, and stepped upon the roof. While he stood there, we could see him plainly, a dark form against a lurid background, as with a few swift strokes he cut a hole in the roof, perhaps a foot from the edge.

The hook was lifted once more, and its point settled

into the place thus prepared for it. The pole that formed
the handle of the hook reached in a long slope nearly to
the ground, and a heavy rope formed a continuation of
it. At the order of the foreman, something like a hundred men seized this rope and stretched themselves out
in line for a big pull. At the same time, some of the
firemen near the building, seeing the first tongues of
flame leap out of the window nearest to the ladder,— for
the fire had somehow got into this wooden building also,
— hastily pulled down the ladder, leaving Monkey standing on the roof, with no apparent means of escape.

A visible shudder ran through the crowd, followed by
shouts of " Raise the ladder again ! "

The ladder was seized by many hands, but in a minute
more it was evident that it would be useless to raise it,
for the flames were pouring out of every window, and nobody could have passed up or down it alive.

" Stand from under ! " shouted Monkey, and threw
his axe to the ground.

Then, getting cautiously over the edge, he seized the
hook with both hands, threw his feet over it, thus swinging his body beneath it, and came down the pole and the
rope hand over hand, like his agile namesake, amid the
thundering plaudits of the multitude.

As soon as he was safely landed, the men at the rope
braced themselves for a pull, and with a " Yo, heave,
ho ! " the whole side of the building was torn off and

came over into the street with a deafening crash, while a vast fountain of fire arose from its ruins, and the crowd swayed back as the heat struck upon their faces.

By this time the engines had got into position, stretched their hose, and were playing away vigorously. The foremen were sometimes bawling through their trumpets, and sometimes battering them to pieces in excitement. The men that held the nozzles and directed the streams were gradually working their way nearer and nearer to the buildings, as the water deadened portions of the fire and diminished the heat. And, through all the din and uproar, we could hear the steady, alternating thud of the brakes as they struck the engine-boxes on either side. Occasionally this motion on some particular engine would be quickened for a few minutes, just after a vigorous oration by the foreman; but it generally settled back into the regular pace.

And now a crack appeared in the front wall of one of the tall brick buildings, near the corner, running all the way from ground to roof. A suppressed shout from the crowd signified that all had noticed it, and served as a warning to the hose-men to look out for themselves.

The crack grew wider at the top. The immense side wall began to totter, then hung poised for a few breathless seconds, and at last broke from the rest of the building and rushed down to ruin.

It fell upon the burning wreck of the wooden structure, and sent sparks and fire-brands flying for scores of yards in every direction.

The hose-men crept up once more under the now dangerous front wall, and sent their streams in at the windows, where a mass of living flame seemed to drink up the water as fast as it could be delivered, and only to increase thereby.

It might have been ten minutes, or it might have been an hour, after the falling of the side wall,— time passes so strangely during excitement,— when another great murmur from the crowd announced the trembling of the front wall. The hose-men were obliged to drop the nozzles and run for their lives.

After the preliminary tremor which always occurs, either in reality or in the spectator's imagination, the front wall doubled itself down by a diagonal fold, breaking off on a line running from the top of the side wall still standing to the bottom of the one that had fallen, and piling itself in a crumbled mass, out of which rose a great cloud of dust from broken plaster.

The two other brick buildings, notwithstanding thousands of gallons of water were thrown into them, burned on fiercely till they burned themselves out. But no more walls fell, and, for weeks afterward, the four stories of empty and blackened ruin towered in a continual menace above their surroundings.

The old shanty which Monkey Roe had hoped would

burn, had been saved by the unwearied exertions of the firemen, who from the moment the engines were in action had kept it continually wet.

" The best of the fire was over," as an habitual fire-goer expressed it, the crowd was thinning out, and Phaeton and I went to look for Ned, who, poor fellow ! was pining in a dungeon where he could only look through iron bars upon a square of reddened sky.

We had hardly started upon this quest when several church-bells struck up a fresh alarm, and the news ran from mouth to mouth that there was another fire ; but nobody seemed to know exactly where it was.

" Let 's follow one of the engines," said Phaeton ; and this time we cast our lot with Rough-and-Ready Seven — not with hand on the drag-ropes to assist in jumping her, but rather as ornamental tail-pieces.

" I think I shall take an axe this time," said Phaeton, as we ran along.

" I 've no doubt you could handle one as well as Monkey Roe," said I,—" that is,"— and here I hesitated somewhat, " if you had on an easy suit of clothes. Mine seem to be a little too tight to give perfectly free play to your arms."

" Oh, as to that," said Phaeton, who had fairly caught the fireman fever, "if I find the coat too tight, I can throw it off."

The new fire proved to be at Mr. Glidden's house. It

had probably caught from cinders wafted from the great fire and falling upon the steps. All about the front door was in a blaze.

At the sight of this, Phaeton seemed to become doubly excited. He rushed to the Hook-and-Ladder carriage, and came back in a minute with an axe in his hand and a fireman's hat on his head, which proved somewhat too large for him, and gave him the appearance of the victorious gladiator in Gérôme's famous picture.

He seemed now to consider himself a veteran fireman, and, without orders from anybody, rushed up to the side door and assaulted it vigorously, shivering it, with a few blows, into a mass of splinters.

He passed in through the wreck, and, for a few minutes, was lost to sight. I barely caught a glimpse of a man passing in behind him. What took place inside of the house, I learned afterward.

Miss Glidden had been sitting up reading "Ivanhoe," and had paid no attention to the great fire, except to look out of the window a few minutes on the first alarm. Hearing this thundering noise at the door, she stepped to the head of the stairs, in a half-dazed condition, and saw ascending them, as she expressed it, "a grotesque creature, in tight clothes, wearing an enormous mediæval helmet, and bearing in his hand a gleaming battle-axe." She could only think him the ghost of a Templar, screamed, and fainted.

"THIS MUST BE PUT IN A SAFE PLACE."

The man who had gone in after Phaeton, passed him on the stairs, and soon emerged from the house, bearing the young lady in his arms. It was Jack-in-the-Box.

Phaeton came out a few minutes later, bringing her canary in its cage.

"This must be put in a safe place," said he to me; "Miss Glidden thinks the world of it. I'll run home with it, and come back again." And he ran off, just escaping arrest at the hands of a policeman who thought he was stealing the bird, but who was not able to run fast enough to catch him.

Meanwhile the firemen were preparing to extinguish the new fire. There was no water-supply near enough for a single engine to span the distance. Some of them had been left at the great fire, to continue pouring water upon it, while the chief engineer ordered four of them to take care of this one.

They formed two lines, Red Rover Three and Big Six taking water from the canal and sending it along to Cataract Eight and Rough-and-Ready Seven, who threw it upon the burning house.

As Phaeton, Jack-in-the-Box, Miss Glidden, and the canary emerged from the house, half a dozen men rushed in — some of them firemen, and some citizens who had volunteered their help. In a little while, one of them appeared at an upper window, having in his hands a large looking-glass with an elaborately carved frame. Without

10*

stopping to open the window, he dashed the mirror
through sash, glass, and all, and as it struck the ground it
was shivered into a thousand fragments.

Then another man appeared at the window with an
armful of small framed pictures, and, taking them one at
a time by the corner, " scaled " them out into the air.

Then the first man appeared again, dragging a mattress. Resting this on the window-sill, he tied a rope
around it, and let it down slowly and carefully to the
ground.

The second man appeared again in turn ; this time
with a handsome china wash-bowl and pitcher, which he
sent out as if they had been shot from a cannon.   In falling, they just escaped smashing the head of a spectator.
Bearing in mind, I suppose, the great mercantile principle
that a " set " of articles should always be kept together,
he hurriedly threw after them such others as he found on
the wash-stand,— the cake of soap striking the chief engineer in the neck, while the tall, heavy slop-jar — hurled
last of all to complete the set — turned some beautiful
somersaults, emptying its contents on Lukey Finnerty,
and landed in the midst of a table full of glassware which
had been brought out from the dining-room.

Next appeared, at another upper window, two men
carrying a bureau that proved to be too large to go
through.   With that promptness which is so necessary in
great emergencies, one of the men instantly picked up his

axe, and, with two or three blows, cut the bureau in two
in the middle, after which both halves were quickly bun-
dled through the window and fell to the ground.

The next thing they saved was a small, open book-
case filled with handsomely bound books. They brought
it to the window, with all the books upon it, rested one
end on the sill, and then, tripping up its heels, started it
on the hyperbolic curve made and provided for projectiles
of its class. If the Commissioner of Patents could have
seen it careering through the air, he would have rejected
all future applications for a monopoly in revolving book-
cases. When it reached the ground, there was a general
diffusion of good literature.

They finally discovered, in some forgotten closet, a
large number of dusty hats and bonnets of a by-gone day,
and came down the stairs carefully bringing a dozen or
two of them. Close behind them followed the other two,
one having his arms full of pillows and bolsters, while the
other carried three lengths of old stove-pipe.

" We saved what we could," said one, with an evident consciousness of having done his duty.

" Yes," said another, " and it 's too hot to go back
there, though there 's lots of furniture that has n't been
touched yet."

" What a pity !" said several of the bystanders.

Meanwhile the Hook-and-Ladder company had fastened one of their great hooks in the edge of the roof,

and were hauling away with a " Yo, heave, ho ! " to pull
off the side of the house. They had only got it fairly
started, separated from the rest of the frame by a crack of
not more than five or six inches, when the chief engineer came up and ordered them to desist, as he expected
to be able to extinguish the fire.

And now the engines were in full play. A little trap-
door in the top of Cataract Eight's box was open, and
the assistant foreman of Red Rover Three was holding in
it the nozzle of Three's hose, which discharged a terrific
stream.

The same was true of Big Six and Rough-and-Ready
Seven.

I never heard a more eloquent orator than the foreman of Cataract Eight, as he stood on the box of his engine, pounded with his trumpet on the air-chamber, and
exhorted the men to " down with the brakes ! " " shake
her up lively ! " " rattle the irons ! " " don't be washed ! "
etc., all of which expressions seemed to have one meaning, and the brakes came down upon the edges of the
box like the blows of a trip-hammer, making the engine
dance about as if it were of pasteboard.

The foreman of Red Rover Three was also excited,
and things in that quarter were equally lively.

For a considerable time it was an even contest.
Eight's box was kept almost full of water, and no more ;
while it seemed as if both companies had attained the ut-

most rapidity of stroke that flesh and bones were capable of, or wood and iron could endure.

But at last four fresh men, belonging to Red Rover Three, who had been on some detached service, came up, leaped upon the box, and each putting a foot upon the brakes, added a few pounds to their momentum.

The water rose rapidly in Eight's box, and in about a minute completely overflowed it, drenching the legs of her men, and making everything disagreeable in the vicinity.

A shout went up from the bystanders, and Three's men instantly stopped work, took off their hats, and gave three tremendous cheers.

We had washed her.

Big Six was trying to do the same thing by Rough-and-Ready Seven, and had almost succeeded when the hose burst. Phaeton and I were standing within a step of the spot where it gave way, and we ourselves were washed.

" Let's go home," said he, as he surrendered his axe and fire-hat to a Hook-and-Ladder man.

" Yes," said I, " it's time. They 've poured water enough into that house to float the Ark, and all the best of the fire is over."

As we left the scene of our labors, I observed that my Sunday coat, besides being drenched, was split open across the back.

"Phaeton," said I, "you forgot to throw off my coat when you went to work with the axe, did n't you?"

"That 's so," said he. "The fact is, I suppose I must have been a little excited."

"I 've no doubt you were," said I. "Putting out fires and saving property is very exciting work."

CHAPTER XVI.

A NEW FIRE-EXTINGUISHER.

IT was not yet morning, and my rope-ladder was still hanging out when Phaeton and I reached the house. We climbed up, and as soon as he could tie up his wet clothes in a bundle, he went down again and ran home.

When our family were assembled at the breakfast-table, I had to go through those disagreeable explanations which every boy encounters before he arrives at the age when he can do what he pleases without giving a reason for it. At such a time, it seems to a boy as if those who ought to sympathize with him, had set themselves up as determined antagonists, bringing out by questions and comments the most unfavorable phase of everything that has happened, and making him feel that, instead of a misfortune to be pitied, it was a crime to be punished. Looking at it from the boy's side, it is, perhaps, wisest to consider this as a necessary part of man-making discipline; but, from the family's side, it should appear, as it is, a cowardly proceeding.

It was in vain that I strove to interest our family with vivid descriptions of how we jumped Red Rover Three, how we washed Cataract Eight, and how we saved Mr. Glidden's property. I suppose they were deficient in imagination ; they could realize nothing but what was before them, visible to the physical eye ; their minds continually reverted to the comparatively unimportant question as to how my clothes came to be in so dreadful a condition. As if 't was any fault of mine that Big Six's hose burst, or as if I could have known that it would burst at that particular spot where Phaeton and I were standing.

The only variation from this one-stringed harp was when they labored ingeniously to make it appear that the jumping, the washing, and the saving would all have been done quite as effectually if I had been snug in bed at home.

Phaeton came over to tell me that Ned was missing.

" I don't wonder that we did n't happen to run across him in that big crowd," said he ; " but I should n't think he 'd stay so long as this. Do you suppose anything can have happened to him ? "

" What could happen ? " said I.

" He may have taken an axe, and ventured too far into some of the burning buildings," said Phaeton.

" No," said I, after a moment's consideration ; " that would n't be like Ned. He might be very enthusiastic about taking care of the fire, but he would n't forget to take care of himself. However, I 'll go with you to look for him."

As we went up the street, we came upon Patsy Rafferty and Teddy Dwyer, pushing Phaeton's car before them, with Jimmy the Rhymer in it. They were taking him out to see what remained of the fire. Jimmy said he was getting well rapidly, and expected soon to be about again on his own legs.

His parents never knew who paid the doctor's bill, but thought it must have been the unknown gentleman who was calling him to come across the street when he was run over.

A few rods farther on, we met Ned Rogers walking toward home.

"Hello! Where have you been all this time?" said Phaeton.

"Can't you tell by the feathers?" said Ned.

"What feathers?"

"Jail-bird feathers. I 've been locked up in jail all night."

Of course we asked him how that came about, and Ned told us the story of his captivity, which the reader already knows.

"But how did you get out?" said Phaeton.

"Why, when 'Squire Moore came to the office and opened the court, I was brought out the first one. And when I told him my story and whose boy I was, he said of course I was; he 'd known Father too many years not to be able to tell one of his chickens as soon as it peeped.

He advised me not to meddle any more with burglar things, and then told me to go home. 'Squire Moore's the 'squire for my money! But as for that stupid policeman, I'll sue him for false imprisonment, if Aunt Mercy will let me have the funds to pay a lawyer."

"Aunt Mercy's pretty liberal with you," said Phaeton, "but you may be sure she'll never give you any such amount as that."

When Ned heard of our adventures at the fire, he fairly groaned.

"It would be just like my luck," said he, "if there should n't be another good fire in this town for a year."

The lost brother being found, Phaeton said the next thing to be done was to take home the bird he had rescued. I went with him on this errand. As we approached the house, Phaeton carrying the cage, a scene of desolation met our eyes. Nearly everything it contained had been brought out-of-doors, and had sustained more or less injury. The house itself, with all the windows and doors smashed out, the front burned to charcoal, the side so far wrenched apart from the rest of the frame that it could not be replaced, and the whole browned with smoke and drenched with water, was a melancholy wreck.

Mr. Glidden and his son John stood in the yard looking at it, and their countenances, on the whole, were rather sorrowful.

" Good-morning, Mr. Glidden," said Phaeton.

" Good-morning, sir."

" I should like to see Miss Glidden," said Phaeton.

" She is at her aunt's, over on West street," said Mr. Glidden.

Phaeton seemed a little disappointed.

" I 've brought home her bird," said he. " I carried it out when the house was on fire, and took it up to our house for safety."

" My sister will be very much obliged to you," said John Glidden. " I 'll take charge of it."

Phaeton intimated his entire willingness to run over to West street with the bird at once, saying that he knew the house where she was staying perfectly well ; but John said he would n't trouble him to do that, and took the cage, which Phaeton gave up with some appearance of reluctance.

" I don't believe the smell of smoke will be good for that bird," said Phaeton, as we walked away. " Canaries are very tender things. He 'd better have let me carry it right over to his sister."

" Yes," said I, " and relieve her anxiety of mind about it. But I suppose he and his father are thinking of nothing but the house."

" I don't wonder at that," said Phaeton. " It must be a pretty serious thing to have your house and furniture knocked to pieces in that way. And the water seems to do as much harm as the fire."

" Yes, and the axes more than either," said I. " But it
can't be helped. Houses will get on fire once in a while, and
then, of course, they must either be put out or torn down."

" I am inclined to think it can be helped," said Phaeton. " I 've been struck with an idea this morning, and
if it works out as well as I hope, I shall be able to abolish
all the engines and axe-men, and put out fires without
throwing any water on them."

" That would be a tremendous invention," said I.
" What is it ? "

" Wait till I get it fully worked out," said he, " and
then we 'll talk it over. It needs a picture to explain it."

A day or two afterward, Phaeton asked me to go with
him to see Jack-in-the-Box, as he had completed his invention, and wanted to consult Jack about it.

" By the way," said he, as we were walking up the
street, " I received something this morning which will interest you."

He took from his pocket, and handed me, a note
written on delicate scented paper and folded up in a
triangle. It was addressed to " Dear Mr. Rogers," and
signed " V. Glidden." It acknowledged the receipt of
the bird, and thanked him handsomely for his " gallantry
in rescuing dear little Chrissy from the flames."

" That 's beautiful," said I, as I folded it up and
handed it back to Phaeton, who read it again before putting it into his pocket.

" Yes," said he, " that's lovely."

" You never were called ' Mr. Rogers ' before, were you ? " said I.

" No," said he.

" I tell you what 't is, Fay," said I, " we're getting along in life."

" Yes," said he ; " youth glides by rapidly. It was only a little while ago that we had never run with a machine, never taken an axe at a fire, and — never received a note like this."

" And now," said I, " we — that is, you — have made an invention to abolish all fire departments."

" If it works," said Phaeton.

" I have n't the least doubt that it will," said I, although I had not the remotest idea what it was.

Jack, who had just flagged a train, and was rolling up his flag as we arrived, cordially invited us into his box.

" I want to consult you about one more invention," said Phaeton, " if you 're not tired of them."

" Never tired of them," said Jack. " I have found something to admire in every one you 've presented, though they were not all exactly practicable. The only way to succeed is to persevere."

" It 's very encouraging to hear you say so," said Phaeton. " The thing that I want to consult you about to-day is a method of putting out fires without throwing water upon the houses or chopping them all to pieces."

"That would be a great thing," said Jack. "How do you accomplish it?"

"By smothering them," said Phaeton.

"I know you can smother a small fire with a thick blanket," said Jack, "but how are you going to smother a whole house, when it is in a blaze?"

"If you will look at this drawing," said Phaeton, "you will easily understand my plan." And he produced a sheet of paper and unfolded it.

"I first build a sort of light canvas tent," he continued, "somewhat larger than an ordinary house. It has no opening, except that the bottom is entirely open, and there is a long rope fastened to each of the lower corners. Then I have a balloon, to which this tent is fastened in place of a car. Of course the balloon lifts the tent just as far as the ropes — which are fastened to something — will let it go."

"That's plain enough," said Jack.

"Then," continued Phaeton, "whenever a fire occurs, the firemen (it needs only a few) take these ropes in their hands and start for the fire, the tent and balloon sailing along over their heads. When they get there, they let it go up till the bottom of the tent is higher than the top of the burning house, and then bring it down over the house, so as to inclose it, and hold the edge close against the surface of the ground till the fire is smothered."

"I see," said Jack; "the theory certainly is perfect."

"I have not forgotten," said Phaeton, "that the tent itself might take fire before they could fairly get it down

PHAETON'S DRAWING.

over the house. To prevent that, I have a barrel of water at this point,— below the balloon and above the tent,— and have a few gimlet-holes in the bottom of the barrel ; so that there is a continual trickle, which just keeps the tent too wet to take fire easily."

" That 's as clear as can be," said Jack. "It 's the wet-blanket principle reduced to scientific form."

" And how shall I manage it ? " said Phaeton.

" As to that," said Jack, " the most appropriate man to consult is the chief engineer."

CHAPTER XVII.

HOW A CHURCH FLEW A KITE.

As soon as possible, Phaeton went down town with his drawing in his pocket, and hunted up the office of the chief engineer. This, he found, was in the engine-house of Deluge One,—a carpeted room, nearly filled with arm-chairs, having at one end a platform, on which were a sofa and an octagonal desk. The walls were draped with flags, and bore several mottoes, among which were "Ever Ready," "Fearless and Free," and "The Path of Duty is the Path of Glory." Under the last was a huge silver trumpet, hung by a red cord, with large tassels.

This was the room where the business meetings of Deluge One were held, and where the chief engineer had his office. But the young men who were now playing cards and smoking here, told Phaeton the chief engineer was not in, but might be found at Shumway's.

This was a large establishment for the manufacture of clothing, and when Phaeton had finally hunted down his man, he found him to be a cutter,—one of several who stood at high tables and cut out garments for the other tailors to make.

11

" I 've come to consult you about a machine," said
Phaeton.

" How did you happen to do that ? " said the chief
engineer, without looking up.

" A friend of mine — a railroad man — advised me to,"
said Phaeton.

" Clever fellers, them railroad men," said the chief
engineer ; " but what 's your machine for ? "

" For putting out fires," said Phaeton.

" One of them gas arrangements, I suppose," said the
chief engineer,—" dangerous to the lives of the men, and no
good unless applied in a close room before the fire begins."

" I don't know what you mean by that," said Phaeton ; " but there 's no gas about mine."

The chief engineer, who all this time had gone on cutting, laid down his shears on the pattern.

" Let 's see it," said he.

Phaeton produced his drawing, spread it out before
him, and explained it.

" Why, boy," said the chief engineer, " you could n't —
and yet, perhaps, you could — it never would — and still it
might — there would be no — but I 'm not so sure about
that.   Let me study this thing."

He planted his elbows on the table, each side of the
drawing, brought his head down between his hands,
buried his fingers in the mass of his hair, and looked
intently at the picture for some minutes.

" Where did you get this ? " said he, at last.

" I drew it," said Phaeton ; " it 's my invention."

" And what do you want me to do about it ? "

" I thought perhaps you could help me in getting it into use."

" Just so ! Well, leave it with me, and I 'll think it over, and you can call again in a few days."

Phaeton did call again, and was told that the chief engineer was holding a meeting in the engine-house. Going over to the engine-house, he found it full of men, and was unable to get in. The next time he called, the chief engineer told him he " had n't had time to look it over yet." Next time he was " not in." And so it seemed likely to go on forever.

But meanwhile something else took place, which called out Phaeton's inventive powers for exercise in another direction.

It happened that the pastor of the Baptist church, in talking to the Sunday-school, dwelt especially on Sabbath-breaking, and mentioned kite-flying as one of the worst forms of it.

" This very day," said he, " as I was coming to church, I saw three wicked boys flying kites in the public street, and one of them sits in this room now."

A boy who knew whom the pastor referred to, pointed out Monkey Roe.

As many of the school as could, turned and stared at

Monkey.   The truth was, he had not been flying a kite ;
but on his way to church he passed two boys who were.
It was the universal practice — at that time and in that
country, at least — when a boy was flying a kite, for every
other boy who passed to ask "how she pulled?" and
take the string in his hand a moment to see.

If she pulled hard, the flyer was rather proud to have
his friends ask the question and make the test.   In fact, I
suppose it would hardly have been polite not to ask.

Monkey had just asked this interesting question, and
had the string in his hand, when the pastor happened to
pass by and see the group.   Of course it would have
been well if he could have stood up in the Sunday-school,
and simply told the fact.   But he was not the sort of boy
who could do such a thing at any time, and he was especially unable to now, when he was taken by surprise, and
felt that an outrage had been committed against his character and reputation.

But perhaps the pastor was not much at fault.   He
had probably been born and brought up in a breezeless
country where kite-flying was unknown, and therefore
was ignorant of its amenities.

Just before the school closed, Monkey was struck with
a mischievous idea.

"I prophesy," said he to the pastor's son, who sat
next to him, "that this church will fly a kite all day next
Sunday."

"I should be greatly delighted to see it," answered the pastor's son.

Early Monday morning, Monkey went over to Dublin, and found Owney Geoghegan, who had chased and recovered one of the kites that drew Phaeton's car. Monkey obtained the kite, by trading a jack-knife for it, and carried it home. Every day that week, as soon as school was out, he took it to a large common on the outskirts of the town, and flew it. He thoroughly studied the disposition of that kite. He experimented continually, and found just what arrangement of the bands would make it pull most evenly, just what length of tail would make it stand most steadily, and just what weight of string it would carry best.

It occurred to him that an appropriate motto from Scripture would look well, and he applied to Jack-in-the-Box for one, taking care not to let him know what he wanted it for. Jack suggested one, and Monkey borrowed a marking-pot and brush, and inscribed it in bold letters across the face of the kite.

Finally he procured a good ball of string, a long and strong fish-line, and a small, flat, light wooden hoop, which he carefully covered with tin-foil, obtained at the tobacco-shop.

Saturday night Monkey's mother knew he was out, but not what he was about, and wondered why he stayed so late. If she had gone in search of him, she might have found him in Independence square, moving about in a very mysterious manner. The Baptist church, which had a tall, slender spire, ending in a lightning-rod with a single point, faced this square.

It was a bright, moonlight night, and it must have been after eleven o'clock when Monkey walked into the square with his kite, accompanied by Owney Geoghegan.

Monkey laid the kite flat on the ground near one corner of the square, stationed Owney by it, and then walked slowly to the opposite corner, unwinding the string as he went.

After looking around cautiously and making sure that nobody was crossing the square, he raised his hand and gave a silent signal. Owney hoisted the kite, Monkey ran a few rods, and up she went. He rapidly let out the entire ball of string, and she sailed away into space till she hovered like a night-hawk over the farthest corner of the sleeping city.

The Sunday-school room was hung round with mottoes, printed on shield-shaped tablets, and Monkey had made copies of some of them on similarly shaped pieces of paper, which he fastened upon the string at intervals as he let the kite up.

Among them I remember " Look aloft ! " " Time flies ! " and " Aspire ! "

Then Monkey took up the hoop, and tied the string through a hole that was bored near one edge. Through a similar hole on the opposite side of the hoop, and near the same edge, he tied about a yard of comparatively weak string. To the end of this he tied his long fish-line, which he carefully paid out. The kite sailed still higher and farther away, of course carrying the hoop up into mid-air, where it was plainly visible as the tin-foil glittered in the moonlight.

So far, Monkey's task had all been plain mechanical work, sure of success if only performed with care. But now he had arrived at the difficult part of it, where a great amount of patience and no little sleight-of-hand were necessary. The thing to be done was, to let out just enough string for the kite to carry the hoop exactly as high as the top of the steeple.

It took a vast deal of letting out, and winding in, walking forward, and walking backward, to accomplish this, but at last it seemed to be done. Then he must walk back and forth till he had brought the hoop not only on a level with the top of the spire, but directly over it, which took more time. As the strings were fastened at one edge of the hoop, of course it remained constantly horizontal.

When, at last, Monkey had brought it exactly over the point of the lightning-rod, he carefully and steadily brought the hand in which he held the string down to the ground. The hoop encircled and slid down the rod, and, after two hours' hard work, his task was virtually done.

He had now only to walk up to the church, and give a steady, hard, downward pull at the fish-line, when the weak piece of string that fastened it to the hoop snapped in two. Winding up the fish-line, he slipped it into his pocket, looked about once more, said good-night to Owney, walked rapidly home, and went softly up to bed.

Sunday morning dawned beautifully, and everybody in town, who ever went to meeting at all, prepared for church. As the time for services approached, the bells rang out melodiously ; down every street of residences, door after door opened, as individuals and families stepped forth, attired in their best, and soon the sidewalks were full of people passing in every direction.

Somebody discovered the kite, and pointed it out to somebody else, who stopped to look at it, and attracted the attention of others ; and thus the news spread. A few groups paused to gaze and wonder, but most of the people passed on quietly to their respective places of worship.

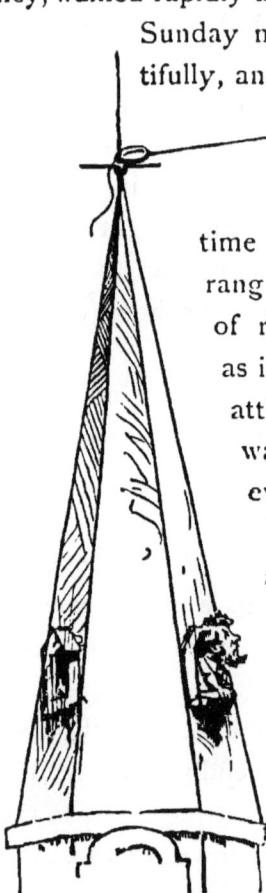

Somebody told the Baptist pastor of it as
he was ascending the pulpit-stairs.

"I will have it at-
tended to,"   said he ;
and,   calling the sexton, he
                    ordered him to go into the steeple
at once and take down the kite.

Easy to say, but impossible to do. The highest point the sexton could reach was more than
forty feet below the top of the spire, and there he could
only poke his head out at a little trap-door. The appearance of his head at this door was the signal for a
derisive shout from a group of boys on the sidewalk.

By the time the services in the various churches were
over, and the people on their way home, nearly everybody in town had heard of the phenomenon. They gathered in small groups, and gazed at it, and talked about it.
These groups continually grew larger, and frequently two
or three of them coalesced. They soon found that the
best point to view it from — considering the position of
the sun, and other circumstances — was the southwest corner of the square ; and here they gradually gathered, till
there was a vast throng, with upturned faces, gazing at the
kite and its appendages, and wondering how it got there.

It was amusing to hear the wild conjectures and grave
theories that were put forth.

One man thought it must have been an accident.

11*

"Probably some boy in a neighboring town," he said, "was flying the kite, when it broke away, and, as the string dragged along, it happened to catch somehow on that steeple."

Another said he had read that in China grown-up people flew kites, and were very expert at it. "Depend upon it," said he, solemnly, "you'll find there's a China-man in town."

Another presumed it was some new and ingenious method of advertising. "Probably at a certain hour," said he, "that thing will burst, and scatter over the town a shower of advertisements of a new baking-powder, war-ranted to raise your bread as high as a kite, or some other humbug."

Still another sagacious observer maintained that it might be merely an optical illusion,—a thing having no real existence. "It may be a mirage," said he; "or per-haps some practical joker has made a sort of magic-lan-tern that projects such an image in mid-air."

Patsy Rafferty happened to see a lady sitting at her window, and looking at the kite through an opera-glass. Immediately he was struck with an idea, and ran off home at his best speed. His mother was out visiting a neigh-bor; but he did n't need to call her home; he knew where she kept his money.

Going straight to the pantry, he climbed on a chair and took down what in its day had been an elegant china teapot, but was now useless, because the spout was broken off. Thrusting in his hand, he drew out the money which the Clown had collected for him from the crowd on the tow-path,— every cent of it, except the crossed shilling, the bogus quarter, the brass buttons, and the temperance medal.

Patsy then ran to a pawnbroker's shop, before the window of which he had often stood and studied the " unredeemed pledges" there displayed.

The pawnbroker, whose Sabbath was the seventh day, sat in the open door, smoking a pipe.

" How much for a spy glass ? " said Patsy, as soon as he could get his breath.

" Come inside," said the pawnbroker. " This one I shall sell you for five dollars — very cheap." And he handed Patsy an old binocular, which really had very powerful glasses, though the tubes were much battered.

Patsy pointed it out of the door, and looked through it.

" Oh, Moses ! " said he, as a dog larger than an elephant ran across the field of vision.

" Sir ? " said the pawnbroker.

" I can't buy it," said Patsy, with a sigh, laying it upon the counter.

" Why not ? " said the pawnbroker.

" I have n't enough money," said Patsy.

" How much have you got ? " said the pawnbroker.

" Three dollars and eighty-four cents," said Patsy.

"And you don't get some more next Saturday night?" said the pawnbroker.

"No," said Patsy.

"Well, you are a good boy," said the pawnbroker; "I can see that already; so I shall sell you this fine glass for three dollars and eighty-four cents,— the very lowest price. I could not do it, but I shall hope that I trade with you again some day."

Patsy put down the money in a hurry, took the glass, and left the shop.

He went to where the crowd was gazing at the kite, took a long look at it himself, and then began renting out the glass at ten cents a look, at which price he found plenty of eager customers.

When they looked through the glass, they read this legend on the face of the kite :

Ye shall have in abomination
the kite after his kind.

LEVIT. XI. 13, 14.

When Teddy Dwyer saw the success of Patsy's speculation, he thought he also had an idea, and running home, he soon reappeared on the square with a large piece of newly smoked glass. But nobody seemed to care to view the wonder through smoked glass, though he offered it at the low price of "wan cent a look," and Teddy's investment was hardly remunerative.

Patsy, before the day was over, amassed nearly thirteen dollars. He carried it all home, and without saying anything to his mother, slipped it into the disabled teapot, where the money collected for him by the Clown had been kept.

The next day he quietly asked his mother if he might have ten cents of his money to spend.

"No, Patsy," she answered, "I'm keeping that ag'in the day you go into business."

But Mrs. Rourke was present, and she pleaded so eloquently Patsy's right to have "a little enjoyment of what he had earned," that his mother relented, and went to get it.

"Either my hands are getting weak," said she, as she lifted it down, "or this teapot has grown heavy."

She thrust her hand into it, uttered an exclamation of surprise, and then turned it upside down upon the table, whereupon there was a tableau in the Rafferty family.

"I often heard," said Mrs. Rafferty, "that money breeds money, but I never knew it bred so fast as that."

She more than half believed in fairies, and was proceeding to account for it as their work, when Patsy burst out laughing, and then, of course, had to tell the story of how the money came there.

"And so you got it be goin' after pawnbrokers, and be workin' on Sunday?" said his mother.

Patsy confessed that he did.

" Then I 'll have none of it," said she, and opening
the stove, was about to cast in a handful of the coins,
when she hesitated.

" After all," said she, " 't is n't the money that 's done
wrong ; why should I punish it ? "

So she put it back into the teapot, and adopted a less
expensive though more painful method of teaching her son
to respect the Sabbath.

In the bitterness of the moment, Patsy firmly resolved
that when he was a millionnaire — as he expected to be
some day — he would n't give his mother a single dime.
He afterward so far relented, however, as to admit to
himself that he might let her have twenty thousand dollars, rather than see her suffer, but not a cent more.

CHAPTER XVIII.

DEACON GRAHAM had predicted that "the wind would go down with the sun," and then the kite would fall. But the prediction was not fulfilled : at least there seemed to be a steady breeze up where the kite was, and in the moon-lighted evening it swayed gently to and fro, tugging at its string, and gracefully waving its pendulous tail. All the young people in town appeared to be walking out to see it, and the evening services were very slimly attended.

Monday morning the trustees of the church began to take vigorous measures for the suppression of the mysterious kite.

The cart of Hook-and-Ladder No. 1 was wheeled up in front of the church, and the two longest ladders taken off, spliced together, and raised with great labor. But they fell far short of reaching any point from which the hoop that held the kite could be touched.

"I hope you are satisfied," said the foreman to the trustees. "I told you them ladders would n't reach it, nor no others that you can get."

"Yes, I see," said Deacon Graham. "I supposed the ladders were longer. But we're very much obliged to you and your men."

"You're welcome," said the foreman, as the men replaced the ladders on the cart. "And by the way, Deacon, if you was thinking of sending a dish of oysters and a cup of coffee around to the engine-house, I may say that my men prefer Saddle-rocks and Java."

"Just so!" said the Deacon. "I'll send Saddle-rocks and Java, if I send any."

One of the trustees suggested that the most muscular of the firemen might go up in the steeple, open the little trap-door, and from there throw clubs at the string.

One of the firemen procured some sticks, about such as boys like for throwing into chestnut-trees, and went up and tried it. But the door was so far below the top of the steeple, and the position so awkward to throw from, that he did not even hit the string, and after one of the clubs in descending had crashed through the stained-glass skylight of a neighboring mansion, this experiment was abandoned.

The next consisted in firing with rifles at the kite, the hoop, and the string. The trustees looked up two amateur huntsmen for this purpose, and furnished a small amount of ammunition.

As there was a city ordinance against discharging fire-arms "in any street, lane, or alley, park, or square of the said city," the trustees were obliged to go first to the Mayor and get a suspension of the ordinance for this special purpose, which was readily granted.

As soon as the two huntsmen saw this in black and white, they fired half a dozen shots. But they did not succeed in severing the string or smashing the hoop. Like all failures, however, they gave excellent reasons for their want of success, explaining to the trustees that there was a difference between a covey of partridges and a small hoop on the top of a steeple. Their explanation was so lucid that I feel confident the trustees must have understood it.

" In rifle-shooting," added one of the huntsmen, " you always have to make allowance for the wind, and we can't tell how it may be blowing at the top of that spire till we learn by experimental shots. But we shall get the range after awhile ; it's only a question of time."

What little ammunition they had with them was soon exhausted, and Deacon Graham, who was very excitable and over-sensitive as to anything connected with the church, rushed down town to buy some more.

" How much powder will you have ? " said the clerk. " Enough to shoot a kite off from a steeple," said the Deacon.

The clerk could n't tell exactly how much that would take — had not been in the habit of selling powder for that purpose.

" Give me enough, at any rate," said the Deacon.

The clerk suggested that the best way would be to send up a small keg and let them use as much as was necessary, the remainder to be returned. To this the Deacon assented, and accordingly a small keg of powder, with a liberal quantity of bullets and caps, was sent up at once,— all to be charged to the account of the church militant.

At the first shot the boys had begun to gather. When they found what was going on, that the ordinance was suspended, and that ammunition was as free as the gospel, they disappeared one after another, and soon reappeared carrying all sorts of shot-guns, muskets, and even horse-pistols and revolvers. No boy who could get a fire-arm failed to bring it out. Most of us had to hunt for them ; for, so far as I know, not one of our boys was guilty of the folly of habitually carrying a pistol in his pocket.

The powder and bullets were on the church steps, where all who wished to aid in the good work could help themselves ; and within half an hour from the time the ball opened, at least thirty happy and animated boys were loading and firing.

The unsectarian spirit of those boys was beautiful to behold. They were from all denominations, and yet every one of them was both willing and eager to burn Baptist powder in firing Baptist bullets at a Baptist steeple.

The noise had attracted the townspeople, and several hundred of them now stood looking on at the strange spectacle.

Patsy Rafferty ran home to draw some money from his teapot-bank, but found the cashier present, and hesitated. However, he soon plucked up courage, and said, with a roguish twinkle :

" Mother, will you please lend me two dollars of my money ? "

Ordinarily, Mrs. Rafferty would have said no. But she was a very bright woman, and was so pleased with this evidence that Patsy had inherited some of her own wit, that she could not find it in her heart to refuse him.

" There 's two dollars, and I suppose when you come back it 'll be four," said she, remembering how money breeds money.

" Yes — four o'clock," said Patsy, as he ran out of the door and made for his friend the pawnbroker's, who sold him an old musket, with which, in a few minutes, Patsy joined the volunteers.

Ned Rogers had not been able to find any fire-arm ; but when he learned where Patsy got his musket, and that the pawnbroker had a mate to it, he ran off to his aunt's house at his best speed, and entering unceremoniously, exclaimed :

" Aunty, I want two dollars quicker than lightning ! "

" Edmund Burton ! how you frighten me," said his

Aunt Mercy. " Jane, get my pocket-book from the right-hand corner of my top bureau-drawer, and throw it downstairs right away."

The instant the pocket-book struck the floor, Ned snatched two dollars out of it and was off like a shot.

" Sweet, benevolent boy ! " said Aunt Mercy. " I 've no doubt he 's hastening to relieve some peculiar and urgent case of distress he has discovered among the poor and sorrowful."

As it was rather late when Ned arrived at the church with his weapon, and the keg of powder was in its last quarter, he thought he 'd make up for lost time. So he slipped in three bullets, instead of one, with his first load, and in his excitement rammed them so hard as almost to weld them together.

The consequence was that, when he discharged it, a large sliver was torn from the spire, and at the same time he found himself rolling over into the gutter, a very peculiar case of distress, indeed.

When Deacon Graham saw how fast the ammunition was disappearing, while the desultory firing produced no effect upon the kite, he thought some better plan should be devised, and conceived of a way in which, as he believed, concerted action might accomplish the desired result. But when he tried to explain it to the crowd, everybody was excited, and nobody paid the slightest attention to him.

The spectators partook of the general excitement, and applauded the performance.

"Bang away, boys! Never mind the Deacon!" said the pastor's son, as he pulled both triggers of a neat little double-barrelled shot-gun.

"*Epigrus via, generosissimi tormentarii !* Peg away, most noble gunners!" shouted Holman.

The Deacon, who had been growing more and more excited, was now beside himself. In his desperation, he sat down upon the keg of powder, and declared that no more should be used till he was listened to. Whereupon the pastor's son produced a lucifer match, lighted it, and declared that if the Deacon did n't get up at once, he 'd send him kiting.

"Get up, or go up," was the laconic way in which he put it ; and the Deacon got up.

"I 'll tell you, Deacon," said one of the huntsmen, " a chain-shot would be the thing to break that string with."

"You shall have it," said the Deacon, and off he posted down town again, to order chain-shot. But the article was not to be had, and when he returned, the kite still rode triumphant.

The trustees held a meeting on the steps of the church. "Now don't get excited," said Mr. Simmons, the calmest of them ; " the first shower will bring down the kite. We 've only to go off quietly about our business, and leave it to nature."

"I don't know about that," said Monkey Roe, in a low tone, to one of the boys who had crowded around to learn what the trustees would do. "The back of that kite is pretty thoroughly greased. It'll shed water like a duck, and nothing less than a heavy hail-storm can bring it down."

"How do you know that, young man?" said Mr. Simmons, who overheard him.

"Why," said Monkey, seeing that he had betrayed himself, "you see — the fact is — I — I — saw a little bird try to light on the kite, but he slipped off so quick I knew it must be greased."

"Humph!" said Mr. Simmons. "That's a likely story."

"Brother Simmons," said Deacon Graham, "we can't wait for a storm,— there is no prospect of any. If we don't dispose of this thing pretty soon, I'm afraid it'll make us ridiculous."

Nobody was able to suggest any means of relief. Perhaps a sailor could have climbed the lightning-rod; but there was no sailor in town, and half way up the spire the rod was broken and a section was missing. There seemed to be no way short of building a scaffolding to the top of the steeple, which would have cost considerable money.

The pastor's son took Monkey Roe aside. "Your prophesy has been nobly fulfilled," said he, "and you've given us a tremendous piece of fun. Get us up another as good as this."

The result of the deliberations of the trustees was, that they resolved to offer a reward of twenty dollars to any one who would get the kite off from the steeple; and this offer was formally proclaimed to the crowd by Deacon Graham.

Hardly had the proclamation been made, when Phaeton Rogers, who had conceived a plan for getting down the kite, and had been preparing the necessary implements, appeared on the scene with his equipment.

This consisted of a powerful hickory bow, about as tall as himself, two heavy arrows, and a large ball of the best kite-string.

After measuring with his eye the height of the steeple and the direction of the kite, Phaeton said he must mount to the roof of the church.

"Certainly, young man," said Deacon Graham; "anything you want, and twenty dollars reward if you'll get that thing down. Here, sexton, show this young gentleman the way to the roof."

Phaeton passed in at the door with the sexton, and soon reappeared on the roof. The crowd seemed to watch him with considerable interest.

Standing on the ridge-pole, he strung his bow. Then he unwound a large part of the ball of string, and laid it out loosely on the roof; after which he tied the end of it to one of the arrows, and laid the arrow across his bow.

A murmur of approbation ran through the crowd, as they thought they saw his plan.

Pointing the arrow upward at a slight angle from the perpendicular, and drawing it to the head, he discharged it. The shaft ascended gracefully on one side of the string of the kite, and descended on the other side.

At sight of this, the crowd burst into applause, suppos-

"POINTING THE ARROW UPWARD AT AN ANGLE, PHAETON DREW IT TO THE HEAD."

ing that the task was virtually accomplished. It would have been easy enough now to take hold of the two ends of the string that had been carried by the arrow, and by simply pulling bring down the kite. But this would not have taken off the hoop from the top of the spire, and it would have been necessary to break off the kite-string, leaving more or less of it attached to the hoop, to float on the breeze like a streamer till it rotted away. Phaeton intended to make a cleaner job than that.

When the arrow fell upon the ground, Ned, by his brother's direction, picked it up and held it just as it was. Phaeton threw down the ball of string still unwound, and then descended to the ground. He very quickly made a slip-knot on the end of the string, passed the ball through it, and then, by pulling carefully and steadily on the ball-end, made the slip-knot slide up till it reached the string of the kite. Before it was pulled up tight, he walked out on the square in a direction to pull the slip-knot as close as possible to the hoop.

This done, he placed himself, with the string in his hand, on the spot where he supposed the one who got up the kite must have stood while putting the hoop over the point of the lightning-rod. That is to say, he walked from the church in such a direction, and to such a distance, that the string he held in his hand formed a continuous and (but for the sag) straight line with the string that held the kite to the hoop.

He expected, on arriving at this point, to raise his hand, give a jerk or two at the string, and see the hoop slide up and off the rod, from the tendency — caused by the kite's pulling at one end of the string, and himself at the other — to take up the sag.

His theory was perfect, but the plan did not work ; probably because the wind had died down a little, and the kite was flying lower than when it was first put up.

When he saw that the hoop was not to be lifted by this means, he cast about for a further expedient, the crowd meanwhile expressing disappointment and impatience.

Carrying the string entirely across the square, he stopped in front of the house that was in line with it, and asked permission to ascend to the roof, which was granted. Breaking off the string, and telling Ned to stand there and hold the end, he put the ball into his pocket, took a pebble in his hand, and went up through the house and came out at the scuttle.

Tying the pebble to the end of the string, he threw it down to his brother, who tied the end of the string to the end he had been holding. Phaeton then drew it up, and once more pulled at the hoop.

It stuck a little at first ; but as he alternately pulled and slackened, it was started at last, and began to slide up the lightning-rod ; whereupon the crowd set up a shout, and a great many people remarked that they knew all the while the boy would succeed.

But the hoop only rose to a point about half way between its former resting-place and the tip of the rod, and
there it remained. No sleight-of-hand that Phaeton could
exercise would make it rise another inch. If the wind
had freshened, so as to make the kite sail higher, the
hoop would have slid to the top of the rod at once. But
the wind did not freshen, and there was no taller building anywhere in line with the string than the one Phaeton
was standing on.

The crowd expressed disappointment again, some of
them groaned, and remarked that they had been confident
all the while the boy could n't do it.

" Ned," said Phaeton, " come up here."

Ned went up.

" Now," said Phaeton, " stand right in this spot ; hold
the string just as you see me holding it now ; and try to
pull on it just hard enough to make the hoop hang loosely
around the rod instead of being held close against it either
by the tugging of the kite one way, or by your pulling
the other."

" I understand," said Ned. " I'll do my best."

Phaeton then went back to the church, and ascended
to the roof again with his bow and arrow and the ball of
string. Laying out the string as before, and tying the
end to the arrow, he shot it over the kite-string so that
the arrow fell upon the roof.

Making a slip-knot as before, he pulled upon the end

of his string till the knot slid up to the kite-string at a point pretty near the hoop. He now broke off the string, leaving it just long enough to reach from the point where it was attached to the kite-string straight down to where he stood on the roof.

He tied the end to his arrow, and, drawing the shaft to the head, shot it straight upward. As the arrow left the bow, the crowd cheered again, for it was evident that when the arrow, in its course, should reach a point as far above the kite-string as Phaeton was below it, it would begin to pull the kite-string upward, and if it had force enough to go a yard or two higher, it must, of course, pull the hoop off from the rod.

But it lacked force enough. It rose till it had almost straightened the string it was carrying, and then wearily turned its head and dropped to the roof again.

The crowd groaned, and some of them left for their homes or their business, saying they knew all the while that foolery would n't work.

Phaeton sat down on the ridge-pole of the church, put his head between his hands, and thought. While he sat there, the crowd shouted all sorts of advice to him, most of which was intended to be sarcastic, though some spoke seriously enough, as those who suggested that he use a larger bow and a lighter string.

After some moments he got up, went to the arrow, and detached it from the string; then, taking the end of the string between his palms, he rolled it and rolled it, until he had very greatly hardened the twist.

If you have ever twisted a piece of common string up tight, and then, taking the two ends between your thumb and finger, let go of the middle, you know what it does. It doubles and twists itself together, in the vain effort to untwist.

When Phaeton had tightened the twist of his string as much as he could, he tied the arrow on again, laid it across his bow, pointed it toward the zenith, drew it to the head, and once more discharged it.

While the arrow was climbing, the string — wherever the slack folds of it hung near enough to one another — was doubling and twisting together, thus greatly shortening itself. The arrow had not gone much more than half its former distance above the kite-string when it arrived at the end of its own now shortened string, and gave such a jerk as pulled the hoop clear up from the end of the lightning-rod.

When the crowd saw this, they burst into a tremendous cheer, threw their caps into the air, and bestowed all sorts of compliments upon Phaeton.

Phaeton took off his hat and made a low bow to the people, and then disappeared through the little door in the tower, by which he had gained access to the roof. He soon reappeared, emerging from the front door, and then ran across the square, to the house where Ned still stood on the roof, like a statue, or Casabianca, waiting for his next orders.

"Haul her in," said Phaeton, and Ned immediately began winding in the kite, using his left forearm as a reel, and passing the string around his elbow and through the notch between his thumb and forefinger. He wound on everything as he came to it — hoop, mottoes, even Phaeton's arrow.

Phaeton stood in the street before the house, caught the kite by the tail as it approached the ground, and soon had it secure. He broke off the string, and Ned came down through the house.

An immense crowd surrounded them, and impeded their progress as they started for home.

"Jump into my carriage; I 'll take you home," said the driver of an open barouche, who had stopped to see the performance, and like everybody else was intensely interested in it.

Phaeton was instantly seized in the arms of three or four men and lifted into the carriage. Then Ned was lifted in the same way and seated beside him. Then the kite was stood up on the front seat, leaning against the driver's back, with its astonishing motto staring the boys in the face. Lukey Finnerty, who had been proudly holding Ned's musket for him, handed it up, and it was placed aslant of the seat between the two boys. The bow, brought by the sexton, was placed beside it, and

RIDING HOME IN THE BAROUCHE.

the carriage then moved off, while a large number of boys followed in its wake, three of them being suspended from the hind axle by their hands, while their feet were drawn up to clear the ground.

"Why is he carrying away that kite?" said Deacon Graham, asking the question in a general way, as if he expected the crowd to answer it in concert. "That belongs to the church."

"*Sic nodus* — not so," said Isaac Holman. "It belongs to him; he made it."

"Ah, ha!" said the Deacon; "I smell a mice, I s-m-e-l-l a mice!"

As the driver had recently procured his new and handsome barouche, and was anxious to exhibit it, he drove rather slowly and took a somewhat circuitous route. All the way along, people were attracted to their windows. As the carriage was passing through West street, Phaeton colored a little when he saw three ladies standing on an upper balcony, and lifted his hat with some trepidation when the youngest of them bowed. The next moment she threw a bouquet, which landed in the carriage and was picked up and appropriated by Ned.

"I am inclined to think," said Phaeton, "that bouquet was intended for me."

"Was it?" said Ned. "Then take it, of course. I could buy one just like it for a quarter, if I cared for flowers. But, by the way, Fay, what are you going to

12*

do with the twenty dollars you 've won? That's considerable money."

"I am going to put it to the best possible use for money," said Phaeton.

"I did n't know there was any one use better than all others," said Ned. "What is it?"

"To pay a debt," said Phaeton.

"I never should have guessed that," said Ned; "and I don't believe many people think so."

As they rode by Jack's Box, Jack, who stood in the door, learned for the first time what Monkey Roe had wanted the Scripture motto for.

They also passed Aunt Mercy's house, and their aunt and Miss Pinkham were on the piazza. Ned stood up in the carriage and swung his hat. Phaeton saluted his aunt more quietly.

"What in the world are those boys doing in that barouche?" said Aunt Mercy.

"I don't know, but I 'll go and find out," said Miss Pinkham, and she ran to the gate and got the story from one of the Dublin boys, who spoke of Phaeton and Ned as "the Rogers boys," without differentiating them, as a scientific man would say.

Miss Pinkham returned to the piazza and repeated the whole story.

"Edmund Burton always was a smart boy," said Aunt Mercy. "I could have predicted he would be the one to get that kite off. He'd find a way to scrape the spots off the sun, if they wanted him to. But I don't see why that stupid brother of his should be stuck up there to share his glory."

When it came to the question of paying the reward, Deacon Graham stoutly opposed the payment, on the ground that Phaeton himself had been concerned in putting the kite on the steeple — or, at least, had furnished the kite — for the very purpose of getting it down as he did. He said " no boy could fool him,— it was too long since he was a boy himself," — which seemed to me a very singular reason.

It looked for a while as if Phaeton would not get the money; but the other trustees investigated the matter, rejected the deacon's theory, and paid the reward.

On their complaint, Monkey Roe was brought before 'Squire Moore, the Police Justice, to answer for his roguery. The court-room was full, about half the spectators being boys.

" What is your name ? " said the Justice.

" I 'm not sure that I know," said Monkey.

" Not know your own name ? How 's that ? "

" Because, my mother calls me Monty, my father calls me James, and the boys call me Monkey Roe."

" I suppose the boys are more numerous than your parents ? " said the Justice.

" Much more," said Monkey.

"And you probably answer somewhat more readily when they call?"

"I'm afraid I do."

"Then," said the Justice, "we'll consider the weight of evidence to be in favor of the name Monkey Roe, and I'll enter it thus on the record."

As he wrote it down, he murmured: "We've often had Richard Roe arraigned in this court, but never Monkey, I believe."

"Now, Monkey, I'm going to ask a question, which you need not answer unless you choose to. Did you, on Saturday night last, between the hours of sunset and sunrise, raise, fly, and elevate one six-cornered paper kite, bearing a motto or sentiment from the sacred book called Leviticus, and tie, fix, anchor, attach, or fasten the same to the lightning-rod that surmounts the spire, or steeple, of the First Church of the sect or denomination known and designated as Baptist, fronting and abutting on Independence square in this city?"

"To the best of my knowledge and belief, I did," said Monkey.

"Please state to the court, Monkey, your motives, if you had any, for this wicked and atrocious act."

In answer to this, Monkey told briefly and clearly the whole story, which the reader already knows, beginning at the point where he "just stopped half a second, Sunday morning, to see how that boy's kite pulled." When he came to the scene in the Sunday-school room, he gave it with a dramatic effect that was well calculated to arouse sympathy for himself.

'Squire Moore had been as much interested as anybody in the kite on the steeple, and had laughed his enormous sides sore when he scanned it and its appendages through Patsy's glass. When Monkey had finished his story, the 'Squire delivered the decision of the court in a little speech.

"I have searched the Revised Statutes," said he, "and have consulted the best authorities ; but I look in vain to find any statute which makes it a penal office to attach a kite to a steeple. The common law is silent on the subject, and none of the authorities mention any precedent. You have succeeded, young man, in committing a misdemeanor for which there is no penalty, and the court is, therefore, obliged to discharge you, with the admonition never to do so any more."

As Monkey left the bar, there was a rush for the door, the boys getting out first. They collected in a body in front of the building, and, when he appeared, gave him three tremendous cheers, with three others for 'Squire Moore,— in which performance the pastor's son was conspicuous.

But when Monkey came to face the domestic tribunal over which his father presided, he found that a lack of precedent was no bar to the administration of justice in that court.

About a week later, a package addressed to me, and bearing the business-card of a well-known tailor, was left at our door. When I opened it, I found a new Sunday suit, to replace the one which had been ruined when Phaeton wore it to the fire. It must have taken about all of his reward money to pay for it.

For years afterward, the boys used to allude to that season as "the summer we had two Fourth-of-Julys." The scars made by the bullets on the steeple were never healed, and you can see them now, if you chance to pass that way.

CHAPTER XIX.

A CONQUEST.

WHEN, at length, Phaeton got an answer from the chief engineer concerning his invention, it seemed rather surly.

"This thing wont do at all, boy," said he. "It can't be made to work on a large scale." And he handed the drawing to Phaeton, and then turned his back to him and resumed his work.

Phaeton thrust it into his pocket, and walked out of the shop, quite crestfallen. When he told us about it, Ned became indignant.

"I don't believe a word of it," said he; "I see through the whole plot. The chief engineer has entered into a conspiracy with himself to crush out your invention, because he knows it would do away with all the fire-engines and hook-and-ladders, and the city would n't need a chief engineer any more, and he could n't draw that nice little salary of a thousand dollars just for running to fires and bossing things.

"I did n't know that the firemen got any pay," said I. "I thought it was only a patriotic duty,— besides all the fun."

"That's just it," said Ned. "The men who do the hard work don't get a cent; but the chief engineer, who has more fun than any of us,— for he can choose the best place to see the fire from, and can order the engines to play any way he likes,— gets a thousand dollars a year."

I thought almost everybody had had a better place than Ned's to see the Novelty Works' fire, but kept my thoughts to myself.

"I'll spoil that job for him," continued Ned.

"How can you do it?" said I.

"By getting Fay's invention patented, and then having it brought before the Common Council at their very next meeting. We might let this city use it free; that would give us a great reputation for patriotism, and bring it into notice, and then we could make all the other cities pay a big price for it."

"Would n't some people oppose it?" said I.

"Yes, the boys would, because it spoils all the fun of fires; and the chief engineers would, because it spoils their salaries; but all the other people would go for it, because it saves millions of dollars' worth of property. The women, especially, would be friendly to it, because it saves the scare."

"What do you mean by that?" said I, not quite understanding him.

"Why, you must know," said Ned, "that when a woman wakes up in the middle of the night and finds the four walls of her room on fire, and the floor hotter than an oven, and the ceiling cracking open, and the bed-clothes blazing, she 's awfully scared, as a general thing."

" I don't doubt it," said I.

" But Fay's invention puts out the fires so quick, besides keeping them from spreading, that it saves all that anguish of mind, as well as the property."

" It seems to me it 's a good plan," said I, referring to Ned's proposal for taking out a patent at once.

" Then we 'll go to Aunt Mercy and get the money right away," said he. " What do you say, Fay ? "

This conversation took place in the printing-office. Phaeton, after telling us the result of his interviews with the chief engineer, had taken no further part in it, but busied himself setting type.

" I 've no special objection," said he, in answer to Ned's question.

" Then let 's have your drawing," said Ned, and with that in hand, he and I set off for Aunt Mercy's.

" I don't feel quite right," said Ned, as we went along, " about the way Aunt Mercy has always misunderstood these things. This time I am determined to make her understand it right."

" You mean to let her know that it 's Phaeton's invention, and not yours ? " said I.

" That 's the main thing," said he. " I 've got a good deal of credit that belonged to him ; but I never meant to take it. She has always managed to misunderstand, somehow, and I could never see any way to correct it without spoiling the whole business."

"But if you tell her that, will she let you have the money?" said I.

"Not so easily, of course," said Ned; "but still Aunt Mercy's a good-hearted woman, after all, and I think I can talk her into doing the generous thing by Fay."

We found Aunt Mercy apparently in an unpleasant mood, from some mysterious cause. But Ned talked away in a lively manner, and when she began to brighten up, he gradually approached the subject which he really had in mind.

"Aunty," said he, sympathetically, "don't you ever feel afraid of fire?"

"Yes, indeed, Edmund Burton," said she. "I'm afraid of it all the time, especially since I've had this new girl in the kitchen. It seems to me she's very careless."

"If your house should take fire in the night, and burn up the stairs the first thing, how would you get out?" said Ned.

"I really don't know," said she. "I ought, by good rights, to be taken out of the window and down a ladder by some gallant fireman. But it seems to me they don't have any such gentlemen now for firemen as they used to. They're more of a rowdy set."

"They're certainly not very gentle," said Ned.

" Did you hear how they knocked Mr. Glidden's house
and furniture to pieces at the last fire ? "

" Yes ; but why were they allowed to do so ? " said
Aunt Mercy.

" That 's it," said Ned. " Somebody, out of all the
people there, ought to have had sense enough to stop
them. As for myself, I was n't there. I was going, but
was detained on the way."

" If you had been, you 'd have stopped them, I 've no
doubt," said his aunt.

" I should have tried to, I hope," said Ned. " And
now, Aunty, I 'd like to show you a little invention for
doing away with all those horrors."

" Something you want me to furnish money to make
a muddle of, I suppose ? " said she.

" Well, yes, if it pleases you," and here Ned produced
the drawing of the fire-extinguisher. " And now I want
to tell you, Aunty, that this is not my own invention, but
my brother's ; and I think it 's about the best that he 's
ever made."

" U-m-m-m," said Aunt Mercy.

Ned then proceeded to explain the drawing.

" It see it all quite plainly," said Aunt Mercy, when
he had finished. " My house takes fire —— "

" I hope not," said Ned.

" The alarm is given, and this thing is brought
out —— "

"Just so," said Ned.

"In about a minute it is clapped right down over the house —— "

"Precisely," said Ned.

"And smothers the fire instantly —— "

"That's it exactly," said Ned.

"And smothers me in it, as well."

Ned was dumbfounded for a moment, but soon came to his senses.

"As to that," said he, "it's to be supposed that you'd run out of the house just before we put on the extinguisher. But the fact is, you've suggested an improvement already. I guess Fay must have inherited his inventive genius from you. Of course we shall have to build the extinguisher with several flaps, like tent-doors, so that if there *are* any people in the house, they can easily escape."

"And you think I ought to furnish that brother of yours the money necessary to make a proper muddle of this thing?"

"I should be glad if you would," said Ned.

"Well," said Aunt Mercy, "there's a piece of his work in the kitchen now. I wish you'd step out and look at it, and *then* tell me what you think."

Ned and I walked out to the kitchen. There stood the skeletons of half a dozen chairs — those from which we had taken the rounds to make our rope-ladder.

"Those look well, don't they?" said Aunt Mercy, who had followed us. "They belonged to my great-grandfather, and were probably not new in his time. I had them stored at your house, and yesterday I sent a furniture man to get them and polish them up for me. He brings them home in this plight, and tells me the mischief has been done recently, for the saw-cuts are all fresh. They were priceless relics; I would n't have taken ten dollars apiece for them; and your brother has ruined every one of them."

Ned was staggered, and I wondered what he would find to say. But he was equal to the occasion.

"Aunty," said he, "Fay did n't do that——"

"Don't tell me, child; nobody but a boy would ever have thought of such mischief."

"Very true," said Ned; "it *was* a boy — two boys — and we two are the ones."

Aunt Mercy turned pale with astonishment. Apparently it had never occurred to her that Ned could do any mischief.

"We sawed out the rounds," he continued, "to make a rope-ladder. But we did n't know the chairs were good for anything, or we would n't have touched them. If there's any way we can put them in again, we'll do it. I suppose we can get them all — except a few that the policeman carried off."

Aunt Mercy was still more confounded. "Rope-ladder "—" policeman "—that sounded like robbery and State-prison.

" Go home, Edmund Burton," said she, as soon as she could get her breath. " Go home at once, and take away out of my house this bad boy who has led you into evil ways."

Ned wanted to explain my innocence ; but I took myself out of the house with all possible haste, and he soon followed.

" It 's of no use," said he. " Aunt Mercy's heavily prejudiced against me."

When all this was told at the Rogers's breakfast-table next morning, Mr. Rogers could not help laughing heartily. He said his sister valued the chairs far above their real worth, though of course that did not excuse us for sawing out the rounds.

" But as for patenting your invention, boys," said he, " you need not trouble yourselves. It has been tried."

" How can it have been tried ? " said Phaeton.

" As a great many others are," said his father. " By being stolen first. The reason why our worthy chief engineer kept putting you off, was because he thought it was a good invention and wanted to appropriate it. He had a model built, and applied for a patent through lawyer Stevens, from whom I have the information. The application was rejected by the Patent Office, and he had just received notice of it when you called on him yesterday, and found him so surly. His model cost him forty dollars, the Patent Office fee on a rejected application is fifteen dollars, and he had to pay his lawyer something besides. You can guess at the lawyer's fee, and the express company's charge for taking the model and drawings to Washington, and then reckon up how much his dishonesty probably cost him."

"But what puzzles me," said Ned, "is the rejection. That's such a splendid invention, I should think they would have given it a patent right away."

"It does seem so," said Mr. Rogers, who never liked to discourage the boys by pointing out the fatal defects in their contrivances ; "but the Commissioner probably had some good reason for it. A great many applications are rejected, for one cause or another."

Phaeton had suddenly ceased to take any part or interest in the conversation, and Ned observed that he was cutting his bread and butter into very queer shapes. One was the profile of a chair ; another was a small cylinder, notched on the end.

As soon as breakfast was over, Phaeton took his hat and disappeared. He went up to his aunt's house, and asked to see the mutilated chairs.

"I think they can be mended," said he.

"Of course they can," said his aunt. "The cabinet-maker can put in new rounds, but those would n't be the old rounds, and he 'd be obliged to take the chairs

apart, more or less, to get them in. I don't want anything new about them, and I don't want them weakened
by being pulled apart. Unless they are the same old
chairs, every splinter of them, that stood in Grandfather's
dining-room, they can have no value for me."

"I think I could put in the old rounds without taking
the chairs apart," said Phaeton; "and if you'll let me,
I'll take one home and try it."

"Try what you like," said Aunt Mercy. "You can't
make them look any worse than they do now."

So Phaeton took up one of the ancient chairs, inverted
it and placed it on his head as the easiest way of carrying
it, and marched home.

His next care was to secure the missing rounds. He
came over to our house and got the rope-ladder, and then
went to the police-station and had the good fortune to recover the piece which the over-shrewd policeman had
carried off as evidence. This gave him the whole twenty-
four rounds, and it did not take him long to select from
them the four that had been sawed from the particular
chair which he had in hand. Ned and I had done our
work hurriedly, and somewhat roughly, and no two were
sawed precisely alike. We had sawed them so that stubs,
perhaps an inch long, were left sticking out from the legs.

Phaeton procured a fine saw, and sawed one of the
rounds in two, lengthwise, thus splitting it in halves, each
of which, of course, had one flat side and one curved side.

Then he sawed in each of the two stubs which had originally been parts of that same round, a notch, or "shoulder," which cut away about half of the stub,— the upper side of one and the lower side of the other,— carefully saving the pieces that came out of the notches.

Then he put the two halves of the round together, as they were before being sawed apart,— except that he slid them by each other, lengthwise, a distance equal to the length of the notches in the stubs.

Now, as he held the reconstructed round in its place in the chair, it just fitted, and there was sufficient overlap on the stubs to make a secure fastening possible. Near

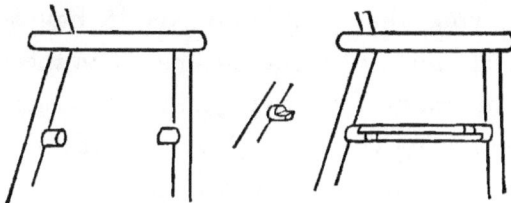

HOW THE CHAIR WAS MENDED.

each end there was a small vacant space, into which the pieces that had been cut out to make the notches in the stubs exactly fitted.

Phaeton procured a pot of glue, and fastened the pieces together and in place. To give the work greater strength, he carefully bored a hole through the stub and the overlapping end of the round, put in a piece of large copper wire, a trifle longer than the hole, and, holding a large hammer against one end, gently pounded on

13

the other with a tack-hammer, till he had flattened it out into a rivet-head ; then reversed the hammers, and made a head on the other end.

Finally, as he had no vise or hand-screws, he placed a strip of wood on each side of the mended round, tied a piece of strong cord in a loose hanging-loop around each end, put a stick through, and twisted them up tight, — the sticks resting against the legs of the chair, which prevented the cords from untwisting. He thus made what a surgeon would call a couple of tourniquets, to hold his work firmly together while the glue was hardening.

Ned and I had watched all these operations with intense interest.

" I tell you what 'tis," said Ned, " Fay sometimes makes mistakes when he goes sailing off in the realms of imagination with his inventive genius, like that fire-extinguisher; but when you come down to a real thing that's got to be fixed, and nobody else can fix it, he's right there every time."

Phaeton treated the other three rounds of the chair in the same manner, and then set it away for the glue to harden. When that had taken place, he took off the tourniquets, scraped and sand-papered the rounds, so as to leave no unevenness at the edges of the pieces, and then varnished them.

Waiting for that varnish to dry was one of the severest

trials of pa-
tience we ever
endured. But
it was dry at
last, and of
course Ned and
I were proud to
go with Phae-
ton when he
carried home
his work.

He left the
chair in the
hall, where
Ned and I also
remained, and
went in first to
speak to his
aunt.

"Seems to
me things are
mightily
changed," said
Ned, in a hu-
miliated tone,

TAKING HOME THE CHAIRS.

"when Fay walks in to see Aunt Mercy, and I stay outside. But I suppose it's all right."

We heard his aunt say to Phaeton :

" I 'd given up looking for you. I thought you 'd find you could n't do it ; but I know you tried hard, poor boy, and I 'm just as much obliged to you."

Presently Phaeton came out and got the chair, and this time we went in with him.

He set it down before his astonished aunt, and carefully explained to her the whole process, showing her that not a splinter of any but the original wood had been used.

That cobbled-up old chair went straight to Aunt Mercy's heart, and seated Phaeton in her affections forever. She made us stay and take tea with her, and after tea we took home the other five chairs, to be similarly treated ; Phaeton marching first with two on his head, then Ned with two more, and I bringing up the rear with the odd one on my head.

CHAPTER XX

PHAETON'S fame as an inventor and general engineer was growing rapidly among the boys. They had great faith in his powers, and in some of them a similar inventive spirit was awakened, though none of them accomplished much. They very commonly came to consult him when they thought they had an idea.

One day Holman came to the printing-office when we were all there,— including Jimmy, who, with the help of Wilson's " Treatise on Punctuation," was learning to read proof,— and said he thought he knew how we could make a fortune.

" That's a good thing to know," said Phaeton.

" But I can't be quite sure that I do know it," said Holman, " till I talk with you about some parts of the scheme."

" I shall be glad to help you if I can," said Phaeton.

" I don't care to make any secret of it," continued Holman, " because, if it can be carried out, we shall have to make a sort of joint-stock company, and take in several of the boys."

"Will it make us a fortune apiece?" said Ned, "or only one fortune, to be divided up among the company?"

"That depends on how much you consider a fortune," answered Holman. "The main thing I want to know, Fay, is this: whether it is possible to invent some way of going under water, and working there, without a big, heavy diving-bell."

"I think," said Phaeton, "that other and lighter apparatus has been invented already; but if not, I should think it could be."

"Then we are all right," said Holman. "I know where the fortune is,— there's no uncertainty about that, — but it's under water a few feet, and it won't do to go for it with any large and noticeable machinery."

"Fay can easily invent a pocket diving-bell," said Ned.

"Do you know the history of Venice?" said Holman.

Phaeton said he knew the outlines of her history, Jimmy said he knew about the Bucentaur and the brass horses, but Ned and I confessed total ignorance.

"I 've just been reading it," said Holman, "and that 's where I got my idea. You must know that when Venice was a rich republic, the Doge — who was the same as a president or mayor — used to go out once a year in a big row-boat called the Bucentaur, with banners and streamers, and a brass band, and a lot of jolly fellows, and marry the Adriatic Sea, as they called it. That is, he threw a splendid wedding-ring into the water, and then I suppose they all gave three cheers, and fired a salute, and had some lemonade, and perhaps made speeches that were a little tedious, like those we have to listen to at school on examination-day. At any rate, he threw in the ring, and that's the important thing."

"What was all that for?" said Ned.

"Jack-in-the-Box told me," said Holman, "it was because the Venetians were a sea-going people, and all their wealth came from commerce, and so this ceremony signified their devotion to the sea. But, as I was saying, this was done regularly every year for six hundred and twenty years; and what makes it lucky for us is, that it was always done at the same spot — the Porto di Lido, a channel through that long, narrow island that lies a little off shore."

"I don't see where the luck for us comes in," said I. "If the Doges had been our grandfathers, and bequeathed us the rings instead of throwing them away, there might be some luck in that."

"Wait till you see what I 'm coming to," said Holman. "The Adriatic is a shallow sea, — I' ve looked up all the facts, — and my idea is, that we might as well have those rings as for them to lie there doing nobody any good."

"How much are they worth?" said Ned.

"You can calculate it for yourself," said Holman. "As I said before, the ceremony was repeated every year for six hundred and twenty years. Of course, we might not get quite all of them — throw off the twenty; there are six hundred rings. They must have been splendid ones, and were probably worth at least a hundred dollars apiece. There's sixty thousand dollars, all in a huddle in that one spot."

"But don't you suppose," said Ned, "that after a while those cunning old Doges would stop throwing in solid gold rings with real diamonds on them, and use brass ones washed with gold, and paste diamonds?"

"I think not," said Holman; "for they did n't have to pay for them — the bill was footed by the Common Council. And they could n't try that without getting caught. For of course the ring would be on exhibition a week or so in the window of some fashionable jewelry store, and the newspapers would tell that it was furnished by the celebrated establishment of So-and-So."

"But don't you suppose," said Phaeton, "that as soon as it was dark, some fellow went out quietly in a little skiff, and dove for the rings? Some of those Italians are wonderful divers."

"I think not," said Holman; "for the ring would be of no use to a Venetian; he would n't dare offer it for sale."

"How do you propose to get them?"

"My plan is, first, to invent some kind of diving apparatus that is small, and can be packed in a valise; then, for us to save up all the money we can get, till we have enough to pay the travelling expenses of two of us from

here to Venice. We could go cheap in a sailing-vessel.
Suppose you and I went, Fay; we'd ask the Venetians
about the fishing, and buy or hire some tackle, and put a
lunch in our valise, with the diving apparatus, and get a
skiff and start off. I've planned the very course. When
you leave the city you steer a little east of north-east;
row about four miles, and there you are."

"That's easy enough," said I,—"only a little over
half the distance from here to Charlotte, which we've all
rowed scores of times."

"When we get there," Holman continued, "we'll
fish a while to lull suspicion, and then I'll quietly get into
the diving apparatus and drop into the water, with the
valise in my hand. It would n't take me long to scoop
up those rings, once I got amongst them; then, of course,
Fay would haul me up, and we'd hurry home and divide.
We could easily turn the rings into money."

"I should think we might get more for them as curi-
osities than as old gold," said I.

"That's a good idea," said Holman.

"But we must n't be in a hurry to sell them *all*," said
Jimmy the Rhymer. "When a fellow grows up and gets
engaged, one of those would be an awful romantic thing
to give to the lady."

"I know a better way than that to get them, though,"
said Ned.

"Let's hear."

13*

"Just invent some kind of magnet that 'll stick to gold, as a common magnet sticks to iron, and put a good strong one in the butt end of your fish-pole ; then, when the Venetians were looking, you could be fishing ; and when they were not looking, you could drop the big end of the pole into the water, poke around a little on the bottom, and haul up a ring. Maybe sometimes you 'd haul up a dozen at once, all sticking together like a cluster of grapes."

Whether Holman was in earnest, or was only testing the credulity of us younger boys, I never knew ; but we took it all in good faith, and went home that night to dream of loading our fingers with rings, and spending sixty thousand dollars divided into five shares. However Holman may have been jesting in this scheme for acquiring a fortune for himself, it was not many days after this when he actually entered upon a rather ludicrous performance to get a little money for somebody else.

There were two Red Rovers in our town — in fact, there were three. The reader has already made the acquaintance of the fire-company and engine known as Red Rover Three. A man who had once belonged to that company, but was now past the prime of life, and honorably retired from the service, made his living by grinding knives and scissors.

But he was too much of a Yankee to go about with a wheel in a little frame strapped upon his back, and a bell in his hand, to be rung monotonously, from street to street.

He built a peculiar carriage,—a square framework, about four feet high and six feet long,—running on four large wheels, wherein was a bewildering mass of machinery. Standing behind it, and laying his hands upon two great brass knobs, he walked slowly through the streets, pushing it before him in a dignified manner, to the awe of the boys and the wonderment of the whole town. It went with an easy motion, the wheels making only a subdued and gentle noise. Surmounting it in front was a large bell, which was struck at solemn and impressive intervals. This apparatus both increased his patronage and elevated the dignity of the profession. He had no vulgar and noisy cry, soliciting custom in a half-intelligible jargon. People who wanted their scissors ground came to the doors with them when they heard his bell. Then the wheels of the chariot stopped, the charioteer lifted his hat in salutation, and the negotiation seemed like a matter of friendly favor, rather than bargain and pay.

In order to grind, he opened a little gate in the rear of the machine, stepped inside, closed the gate behind him, and seated himself upon a small shelf which was fastened to the gate. His feet were then placed upon two pedals, and the machinery began to move.

Five small grindstones, of different sizes and fineness, revolved before him. At his right hand was a little anvil; at his left was a vise; and under this was a box of small tools.

About the middle of the machine, on the top, was a small figure of a Scottish Highlander, with bag-pipes under his arm. The bag — which was of painted tin — was filled with water; and a plug, withdrawn from the longest of the pipes, allowed the water to trickle down upon the knife-wheel. Scissors were generally ground on a dry wheel. When the machinery was in motion, the pipes played something, intended for music, between a squeak and a whistle; so that when he was travelling, the bell rang, and when he was grinding, the pipes played.

On one of the front corners was a little bronze bust of Washington, and on the other was one of Franklin; between them was a clock, with a marine movement.

The whole frame and running gear were painted a bright red, and garnished with shining brass ornaments. The man called his machine Red Rover, after the beloved engine with which he used to run, and the name appeared on the side in brass letters. It seemed as if he must spend the greater part of his earnings on its improvement and embellishment. The man himself, whose hair was broadly streaked with gray, was called "The Old Red Rover," and we never knew him by any other name.

He lived in a little bit of a house by the canal; and the machine, which was always kept in shining order, had to be taken in-doors every night. How he managed to find room in the house for himself, his wife, and his four children, besides the machine, we could never imagine —

and it was none of our business. That little house by the
canal was as much the Old Red Rover's castle as the pal-
aces that you and I live in, dear reader, are ours.

I think it was a week after our conversation concerning the Doge's rings, when, one Saturday, Ned and I
heard the bell ring, and saw the Red Rover coming up
State street, with Isaac Holman propelling it, instead
of its owner.

This was rather astonishing, and, of course, an immediate explanation was demanded.

" Why, you see," said Holman, " Mother had been
for a long time wishing the Old Red Rover would come
around, for every pair of scissors in the house was as dull
as a Dutch grammar. At last she got tired of waiting,
and so I went to his house with them. I found he was laid
up with rheumatism, and had n't been out for five weeks.
It looked to me as if the family were on short rations, and
I began to think what I could do for them. I thought the
best thing would be, to take the machine and spend the
day in going around grinding scissors, and at night take
home the money to the Old Red Rover."

" Yes," said Ned, " that 's the very best thing ; it 's
more fun than anything else you could have thought of."

" He was rather afraid to let me try it," continued
Holman, " but Mrs. The-Old-Red-Rover was greatly
pleased with the idea, and soon persuaded him. ' Be
very tender with her — she 's the pride of my life,' said

he, as we rolled it out of the door; and he did n't mean his wife — he meant the machine."

We had often kept this machine company as it passed through the streets in charge of its owner, and it was doubly interesting now when one of our own number was allowed to run it. So, of course, we went along with Holman on his benevolent tour. Other boys also joined us, and the unusually large crowd attracted attention. We were all ready to explain the situation to people who stood in the doors or looked out at the windows, and the result was that Holman had plenty of work.

Soon after turning into West street, he began to go much more slowly. At the house where Miss Glidden had been living since the fire, nobody appeared at door or window. It happened that right here something got out of order in the machine — at least, Holman said it did, and he had to stop stock-still and tinker at it a long time; but I was not able to see what was out of order.

At last Miss Glidden appeared at the door, and inquired what was going on. Monkey Roe ran up the steps and informed her.

" It 's entirely out of mercy," said he, " and you 'd be doing a benevolent thing to give him as many scissors as possible to sharpen."

Miss Glidden invited him in, and soon collected three pairs of scissors and a pair of shears, which she requested him to take out and have ground for her.

THE BOYS RUN THE RED ROVER.

"Is this all you have?" said he, in a tone signifying that he considered it a very small crop.

"There may be more," said she. "Biddy" — to the servant — "bring here any scissors you have that need grinding."

Biddy brought from the kitchen a pair that were used to trim lamps.

"Is this all, Biddy?" said Monkey.

"I don't know — I'll see, sir," said Biddy; and Monkey followed her to the kitchen.

Next to it he found a sort of combined work-room and store-room, the door of which stood open, and, looking over its contents, soon discovered a pair of tinsmith's shears, a pair of sheep-shears, a drawing-knife, a cooper's adze, and a rusty broad-axe, all of which, with the family carving-knife, brought by Biddy, he added to the collection, and came down the steps with them in his arms.

"Here, Holman," said he, "Miss Glidden wants you to sharpen these few things for the good cause."

"*Boni cani calcei!* — Good gracious!" exclaimed Holman, "does she think I'm Hercules?"

"No," said Monkey, in a low tone, "but I guess she thinks you're Her — admirer."

"But I suppose it must be done," Isaac added, not hearing Monkey's remark. And he took off his jacket and went to work manfully.

The scissors were soon disposed of, as were also the

carving-knife and the drawing-knife ; but the other articles were somewhat troublesome. About all he could do
with the broad-axe was to grind off the rust that completely coated it. The tinsmith's shears were a heavy
job, and the sheep-shears completely baffled him, till
he gave up trying to sharpen them on the grindstone,
and, finding a file in the tool-box, applied that to their
edges, against the solemn protest of Monkey Roe, who
declared it would take the temper out of the steel.

" And when Miss Glidden sees them, it may bring her
temper out too," he added.

" Can't help it," said Holman, " and now the lot 's finished ; you may take it in and collect the pay."

He had just begun to study book-keeping, and, opening a little drawer in the machine, he found a scrap of
paper, and made out this bill :

Miss V. Glidden.
              To Mr. The Old Red Rover.   *Dr.*
To sharpening 3 prs. scissors, @ 6c $0 18
      "   2 " shears, @ 8c 16
      "   1 pr. tinsmith's shears.............. 15
      "   1 " sheep-shears................... 10
      "   1 drawing-knife.................... 8
      "   1 adze 6
      "   1 broad axe......... 20
      "   1 carving-knife.................... 8
                                            _____
                                              $1.01

              Received payment,
                      THE OLD RED ROVER,
                          pr. Holman.

Monkey took this and the armful of cutlery, and carried them in to Miss Glidden, who was somewhat surprised, as she had not known exactly what he was about. However, she laughingly paid the bill, and he carefully piled the articles on the parlor table, and came away.

I observed that Holman put the dollar into the drawer where he had put all the other money, but the cent he put into his pocket. Then he took another cent from another pocket, and threw it into the drawer.

We had travelled perhaps half a mile farther, and Holman had ground something like forty pairs of scissors in all, when we were joined by Phaeton, who watched him as he ground the next pair.

" Is that the way you 've ground them all ? " said he, when it was finished.

" Yes, of course — why ? " said Holman.

" Because if you have, you 've ruined every pair you 've touched," said Phaeton. " Don't you know that scissors must be ground on the edge of the blade, not on the side, like a knife ? If you grind away the sides, the blades can't touch each other, and so can't cut at all."

" I declare, I believe that 's so," said Holman. " I thought it was kind of queer that none of the scissors would really cut anything; but I was sure I had made them sharp, and so supposed they were all old, worn-out things that would n't cut, any way. I guess you 'd better take my place, Fay."

Phaeton declined to do this, but went along as confidential adviser.

We wound about through a great number of streets, the accompanying crowd of boys being sometimes larger and sometimes smaller, and ground a great many knives and scissors.

On turning a corner into a by-street that bore the proud name of Fairfax, we came suddenly upon Jimmy the Rhymer. He was sitting on a bowlder, with a quantity of printed bills over his left arm, a paste-brush in his right hand, and a small bucket of paste on the ground beside him. He looked tired and melancholy.

The outward situation was soon explained. A man who had kept a cobbler's shop for many years, but had recently enlarged it into something like a shoe-store, had employed us to print some bills to be posted up on the fences and dead-walls, announcing the event. They began with the startling legend, printed in our largest type,

GO IT BOOTS!

which was followed by an account of the new store and new goods, the favorite rhetorical figure being hyperbole. Looking about for some one to post them who would do it more cheaply than the regular bill-poster of the town, he had thought of Jimmy the Rhymer, who accepted the job because he wanted to earn a little money.

"Are you sick, Jimmy?" said Phaeton, observing his dejection.

"Not in body," said Jimmy, "but I am sick in mind — sick at heart."

"Why, what's the matter?"

"Look at that," said Jimmy, slowly raising his hand and pointing at one of the bills which he had just posted on a barn-door. "Go it Boots!" — he quoted it very slowly. "What do I care about going it boots? I could n't go it boots if I wanted to. There is no more going it boots for me in this world."

"I don't quite understand you," said Phaeton.

"I mean," said Jimmy, "that my soul yearns for poetry — for the beautiful in nature and art. And it disgusts me to think of spending my time in spreading such literature as this through the world."

"That is n't very complimentary to us," said Ned. "We spent considerable of our time in printing it."

"I suppose you get paid for it," said Phaeton.

"Of course," said Jimmy, "or I should n't do it at all."

"Then it seems to me," said Phaeton, "you might look upon it cheerfully as only so much drudge-work done to purchase leisure and opportunity for the work you delight in. You know a great many famous men have been obliged to get through the world in that way."

"Yes, cheer up," said Monkey Roe. "Look at us:

we 're having lots of fun over drudgier work than yours. Come along with us, and we 'll make one circus of the whole thing — two entertainments under one canvas, as the bills say. Holman has plenty of help, so I 'll be your assistant."

And he took the brush and paste-bucket, while Jimmy still carried the bills, and we all moved on together.

As Jimmy walked beside the machine, he and Holman seemed to resume some former conversation.

"Can't you make up your mind to do it, if I double the price ? " said Holman.

"On the contrary," said Jimmy, "I 've made up my mind that I *wont* do it at *any* price."

" Why not ? " asked Holman.

" For two reasons," answered Jimmy. " One is, that I don't think it 's exactly honest to write such things for anybody else to pass off as his own."

" And the other ? " said Holman.

" The other is," said Jimmy, speaking much lower, but still so that I who was next to him could hear, " and I may as well tell you plainly, Isaac,— the other is, that I have some hopes in that direction myself, and if I write anything more for her, I 'll send it as my own."

" You ? " said Holman, in astonishment.

" Certainly," said Jimmy, with great coolness, as if he felt himself master of the situation, " and I think my claim is better than yours. Whatever there is between

you and her — if there is anything — is entirely of your
seeking. But in my case it's all of her seeking ; she
sent me flowers every day when I was laid up."

"That's nothing — that does n't mean anything,"
said Holman.

"If it does n't, then I 've read the poets all wrong,"
said Jimmy.

"*Poetæ apis suspensi!* — poets be hanged ! " exclaimed Isaac, and then gave a prolonged whistle, which
closed the conversation.

Phaeton, who was next to me, and also overheard,
opened his mouth as if to say something to Jimmy, but
checked himself. Yet he was so full of his idea that he was
obliged to utter it somehow, and so whispered it in my ear :

"If it comes to that, my claim is even better than his, for
she gave flowers to me when I was not an object of pity."

The way Monkey Roe did that job created an epoch
in bill-posting.

We passed the office of a veterinary surgeon, who had
the skeleton of a horse, mounted on a board, for a sign ;
and before anybody knew what he was about, Monkey
whipped off one of the bills from Jimmy's arm, and pasted
it right across the skeleton's ribs.

We came to a loaded coal-cart, broken down in the
middle of the street by the crushing of a wheel, and he
posted one on that.

We passed a tobacco-shop, in front of which stood a life-size wooden statue of a bare-legged and plaided Highlander; and Monkey pasted a Go it Boots! on his naked shin.

We met a beggar who went about on two crutches, but who was known to be an impostor; and after he had passed us, one of the bills was attached to his coat-tail, like the cheapest kind of April-fool.

We passed a windmill that had been put up as an experiment, and had failed; and Monkey posted a bill on each of the sails — revolving it enough to bring each of them near the ground in turn — and one on the door.

There was an omnibus-horse that had fallen by the roadside that morning, and Monkey unfeelingly pasted a Go it Boots! on his poor, dead back.

On whatever he saw that could n't go it at all, he was sure to fasten this advice to go it boots. I think Monkey was a very ironical boy.

" There, Jimmy," said he, as he disposed of the last bill, " you see it 's only necessary to approach your work in the right spirit to make it a pleasure, as the schoolmaster says. But I 'll tell you what to do, if you don't want to spread this sort of literature. The next time Dunderson, or any other cobbler, wants to get out a bill, you write it for him, and put it all in poetry. Then it 'll be a delight to post it."

Jimmy said he 'd consider it.

About five o'clock in the afternoon, when we were all pretty tired, we returned the Red Rover safely to its home, and Holman gladdened Mrs. The-Old-Red-Rover with more money than she had seen in a long time, for which she was very grateful. As we turned away, we met their eldest boy, Johnny The-Old-Red-Rover, bringing a basketful of bark which he had cut from the oaken logs in the saw-mill yard. Before we were out of sight of the house, the smoke curled out of the little chimney, and I 've no doubt they celebrated the day with a joyful supper.

As we passed the Box, we stopped to speak with Jack. He was flagging an express train that was creeping slowly into the city, retarded by a hot box. When it had reached the crossing, it stopped entirely, and most of the passengers thrust their heads out at the windows. One of these heads came out in such a way as to be exactly face-to-face with Jack, the interval between them being less than a yard.

Jack gave a piercing shriek, and fell to the ground.

Phaeton and I ran to him, and picked him up.

"He 's in a fit," said I.

"No," said Phaeton, "I think he has only fainted. Bring water."

I found a pitcher-full in the Box, and we poured it upon his face, which brought him to.

He looked about in a bewildered manner for a moment, then seemed to recollect himself, and turned toward the track.   But the train had passed on.

"Phaeton," said he, "will you please stand here and flag a special freight train that will come along in about ten minutes?"

"Certainly, with pleasure," said Phaeton, receiving the flag.

"And after that has passed, haul down the red ball and run up the white one; then turn that second switch and lock it."

"All right!" said Phaeton.   "I understand."

Jack then picked up his cap, and started on a run, crossing the public square diagonally, evidently taking the shortest route to the passenger station.

CHAPTER XXI.

A TEA PARTY.

THE mending of the chairs had entirely changed Aunt Mercy's demeanor toward us.

" I 've given you money to make a great many muddles," said she ; " but, so far as I can learn, this is the first successful muddle you 've produced. However, this is fine enough to make up for all. And I want you both to come and take tea with me Saturday evening."

Phaeton and Ned not only accepted the invitation with thanks, but asked to have me included in it.

" Certainly," said Aunt Mercy ; " it would n't do to separate you and him. And if you have any other very particular friends among the boys, bring them along too. Only let me know how many are coming."

Phaeton said he should like to invite Jimmy the Rhymer.

" Invite Jimmy," said Aunt Mercy.

" And Monkey Roe is awful lively company," said Ned.

" Invite Monkey," said Aunt Mercy.

" If we 're going to have so many," said Phaeton, " I should n't like to leave out Isaac Holman."

" It is n't exactly a spelling-match, but choose away,"

said Aunt Mercy. " It 's your turn now, Edmund Burton."

Ned chose Charley Garrison, and then Phaeton chose Patsy Rafferty, and after some discussion they determined to let the list end there.   ·

" You have n't mentioned a single girl," said Aunt Mercy.

" Sister May is too little," said Ned ; " and besides that, I don't much believe in girls, any way."

" That 's complimentary to your mother and me," said his aunt.

" I don't think we know any girls well enough to ask them," said Phaeton,— " unless it may be one," and he blushed a little.

" One will do," said Aunt Mercy ; and so it was agreed that she should invite Miss Glidden, whom she called " a very sweet girl."

The evening that had been designated was the evening of the day recorded in the last chapter, and not one of the eight boys included in the invitation forgot it.

We gravitated together, after a series of whistlings, and all went to Aunt Mercy's in a crowd.   ·

When we arrived at the house, Phaeton went up the steps first, and rang the bell. There was no immediate response, and while we were waiting for it, Ned and Monkey Roe, who had lagged behind a little, came up.

" Oh, pshaw ! " said Ned, " don't fool around out

here. Probably the girl's cooking something that she can't leave right away ; but Aunty expects us — come in, boys," and he opened the door and led us into the hall.

"I ought to know the way around this house pretty well," he continued. " Here 's the place to hang your caps," and he pointed out the hat-rack under the slope of the stairs.

With a soft, pattering noise, the eight caps almost instantly found lodgment on the pegs, some being thrown with great precision by the boys who were hindmost over the heads of the others.

" Now follow me, boys ; I 'll introduce you to Aunt Mercy ; I 'm perfectly at home here," said Ned, and throwing open the parlor door, he ushered us in there as unceremoniously as he had admitted us to the house.

The parlor was beautifully though not brilliantly lighted by an argand lamp. Aunt Mercy was sitting on the sofa, and beside her — " awful near together," as Ned expressed it — sat a tall gentleman, with a full beard and a sun-browned face.

" Why! What does this mean ? " said Aunt Mercy, as soon as she could get her breath.

Ned was considerably abashed, and had fallen back so that he was almost merged in the crowd of boys now huddled near the door. But he mustered courage enough to say :

" We 've come to tea."

Phaeton stepped forward, and relieved the situation :

" You remember, Aunty, you asked us to come to tea

this evening, and bring our friends. But, perhaps now it is n't convenient for you. We can come some other day just as well."

"Really," said his aunt, "I made preparations for you to-day, and it 's perfectly convenient; but in the last two hours I had totally forgotten it. You see I have an unexpected visitor."

Phaeton introduced those of the boys whom his aunt had never seen before, and she then introduced us all to Mr. Burton. She had not the least trouble in remembering Phaeton's name, and she called Mr. Burton's attention especially to Ned as his namesake.

"Is this the Mr. Burton who was dead long ago?" said Ned.

"The very same one," said his aunt, laughing. "But he has suddenly come to life again, after many strange adventures, which he has just been telling me. I must ask him to tell them over again for you. But did none of you call for Miss Glidden?"

We all looked blank.

"Then," said she, "Fayette must go after her now."

Phaeton took his cap and started at once. Three of the boys kindly offered to go with him, fearing he would be lonesome, but he said he did n't mind going alone.

While he was gone, we made the acquaintance of Mr. Burton very rapidly. He seemed a good deal like Jack-in-the-Box in one respect — he liked boys. In Ned he appeared to be particularly interested. Several times over he asked him how old he was, and how tall he was. I suppose Ned seemed to him to be a sort of visible measure of the time that had been lost out of his life; for he must have disappeared from the knowledge of his friends about the time that Ned was born.

Soon after Phaeton returned with Miss Glidden, tea was announced.

Both during the meal and afterward, Mr. Burton did the greater part of the talking, and his conversation consisted mainly of a running account of his adventures since he left his home, more than a dozen years before. I give the story as nearly as possible in his own words. It was of a nature to seize upon a boy's fancy; but I fear it has not lain in my memory all these years without losing many of its nicest points.

" I was a tall and slender boy," said Mr. Burton,— " so slender that my parents feared I would become consumptive, and I reached the age of twenty without improving much in that respect. Our family physician said a long sea-voyage might build me up and make a strong man of me, and as my uncle owned a large interest in a whaler then fitting out, at Nantucket, for a cruise in the North Pacific, it was arranged that I should make the voyage. By my own choice, I shipped as a common sailor before the mast, as it seemed to me that was the only way to get the full benefit of the experience.

"I need not tell you the story of the tedious passage around Cape Horn, against head winds and through rainy seas. You have all read it dozens of times. The greenest hand on board was an accomplished sailor by the time we reached the whaling-ground. We had a prosperous cruise, and I calculated that though the hundred and twenty-fifth lay, which was to be my share, would not make me rich, it would give me considerable pocket-money when we got home.

"When we turned our prow southward for the long homeward voyage, our troubles began. Week after week we labored against heavy gales and head seas. It was many months since we had been in port, and we were not well equipped for so long a strain. At last, when we were barely out of the tropics, a terrific and long-continued easterly gale struck us, and drove us helplessly before it. Just before daylight, one morning, she struck heavily, with a shock that sent one of the masts overboard. Dawn showed us that we were wrecked on a lonely island. As nearly as the captain could calculate, this was in south latitude 27° and longitude 110° west.

"We judged that the island must be about a dozen miles long. Three volcanic peaks rose in plain sight, to a height of more than a thousand feet, and between their branching ridges were green valleys sloping down to the shore. If you ever see an old cart-wheel, with half its spokes broken or missing, which has lain upon the ground till the grass has sprung up through it, you may look upon it as a rude representation of the appearance that island presented from the sea. The hub would be the cone of an extinct volcano, the weather-beaten wood being about the color of the volcanic rock, and the remaining spokes the irregular, sharp ridges that radiated from it, some of them reaching to the water's edge and others stopping half-way.

"An hour or two after daylight, we found there was no possibility of saving the ship, though the storm was over. We launched the boats, but could make no landing on that side of the island, which was steep and rocky. So we pulled southward, and through a channel where two rocky islets lay off the south-east point, and soon came to a pretty bay, where we made a landing.

"Looking at the shore through the misty dawn, we had seen what looked like giants standing on the flat roofs of their houses and watching us. But they showed no signs of life, and the captain at length made them out, through his glass, to be images of some sort. We afterward had abundant opportunity to examine them, and found them to be stone statues of colossal size. What we had taken for houses were three platforms of solid masonry, built on ground that sloped toward and overlooked the sea. Four of these great statues had originally stood on each of the platforms, but most of the twelve were now overthrown. We measured one that lay

14*

on the ground, and found it was fifteen feet high and six
feet across the shoulders.

"They were cut in gray stone, and each statue that
was still standing had on its head an immense red stone,
smoothly cut to the shape of a cylinder, at least a yard
high,—as if it wore what you call a band-box hat, but
with no brim. We afterward found there were great
numbers of these statues in various places on the island,
though mostly on the east side. Few of them seemed to
be finished. It was as if the sculptor had taken the
rough blocks and begun work at the top, and, after bringing out the statue perhaps as far down as the waist, had
left it in that condition, and begun on the next one. The
largest one we found was over twenty-five feet high.

" It was two hours after our landing before we saw any
living being. Then we saw three children peeping at us
from the top of a little hill. When we discovered them,
they scampered away, and pretty soon a crowd of people
appeared, led by an old man whose face was painted
white, and who carried a long spear.

"The captain made them understand that we were
cast away, and wished to be taken care of. They led us
along the shore, to the entrance of one of those green
and beautiful valleys, where we found a village and were
made welcome. They kept saying ' *Taya, taya*,' which
we found meant ' friends,' and gave us a feast of yams,
bananas, and roast chicken. The next day they went

through a ceremony which we understood to mean that they formally adopted us into their tribe, and considered us their brothers. They also exchanged names with us. The man who adopted my name (Burton) called it Obuttee, and his which he gave me in exchange was Moancena."

Mr. Burton gave a considerable account of his adventures on the island, which we found very entertaining; but I cannot remember it with sufficient accuracy to attempt repeating it. As we were walking home, Monkey Roe pointed out what he thought were improbabilities in the narrative too great to be believed,—especially the account of the gigantic stone statues, which he said could not possibly have been made by people who had no iron tools. I was inclined to share Monkey's incredulity at the time; but I now know that Mr. Burton told the truth, and that he must have been cast away on Easter Island, where Roggeween, the Dutch navigator, had discovered the mysterious statuary more than a century before.

"That little island," he continued, "was our home for nearly ten years. It is far out of the usual track of ships, and as good water is very scarce upon it, there is little temptation for them to go out of their way to visit it. We had two small boats, but the coast of South America was more than two thousand miles distant.

"At last a merchantman, driven out of her course by stress of weather, came to anchor off the western shore,

and sent in a boat, the crew of which were naturally astonished at being greeted by white men.

"We were taken off, and carried to Melbourne, where
every man took his own way of getting home. About
half of them went to the newly discovered gold-fields. I
got a chance after a while to ship before the mast in a
vessel going to Calcutta.

"There I made the acquaintance of a young man who,
I found, was from my native town; though I had not
known him at home, as he was nearly, or quite, ten years
my junior. His name was Roderick Ayr. He offered to
lend me money, but I would take it only on condition
that he receive my watch as security, to he redeemed
when we reached home. It was a splendid watch,
but had long since ceased to keep time, for want of
cleaning.

"Mr. Ayr had been educated at one of the older col-
leges, knew something of engineering, had studied law,
had spent a year in journalism, and had done a little
something in literature — in fact, I think he told me he
had published a small volume of poems, or essays. His
talents were so varied that he found it difficult to settle down
to one occupation; and so he had made a voyage to India,
merely to see something of the world, while he was growing
a little older and finding out what he was best fitted for

"He was about to return home as a passenger, when
I found an opportunity to ship before the mast in the

'Emily Wentworth,' bound for Boston. To keep me company, he shipped in the same capacity.

"We passed down the Hoogly, and wound through the horrible swamps and jungles of the Sunderbunds, where tigers and crocodiles were an every-day sight, till our pilot left us, on a sunny July morning, with the deep blue waters of the Bay of Bengal before us, and a gentle breeze from the north-east.

"Two days later we were struck by a cyclone, and the vessel was reduced to a helpless wreck. Everybody on board seemed paralyzed with terror, except Ayr and the captain, and the captain was soon swept away by a heavy sea. Three of the men, headed by the second mate, — a fellow named Hobbes,— managed to launch the only boat that had not been stove, threw into it a keg of water, a few provisions, and the charts and instruments, and were about to pull away and leave the rest of us to our fate, when Ayr ordered them back. As they paid no attention to him, he sprang into the boat and took Hobbes by the throat. Hobbes drew his knife, but as quick as lightning Ayr gave him a blow that sent him overboard. One of the sailors caught him and drew him in, and then they all consented to return to the deck. The next sea swept away the boat.

"Ayr was now recognized as commander, by virtue of his natural superiority, and the first mate, a well-meaning but forceless man, had the good sense to resign his authority to the only one who could do anything for us — if anything could be done at all.

" With a few volunteers to assist him, Ayr rigged and launched a raft, upon which nine of us embarked. The remainder of the crew had already been lost, or were afraid to leave the vessel, and some had lashed themselves to her spars. Ayr was the last to leave her. He jumped overboard, swam to the raft, cut the hawser, and we drifted away from the hulk, which heeled and went down before we were out of sight.

" The raft floated low, and half the time we were up to our necks in water, for all that day and all night heavy seas broke over her. Ayr, who was a powerful swimmer, was swimming about the raft the greater part of the time, sometimes tightening the fastenings where she threatened to break apart, and often saving and hauling on board again some poor wretch who had been swept off. But every few hours a man would be carried away whom Ayr could not reach, and our little company was continually growing smaller.

" As for myself, I was rather a poor swimmer, and either the exposure, or some disease that I had previously contracted, caused an uncomfortable swelling and puffiness in my fingers and toes. I took off, with some difficulty, a ring which I had worn for a dozen years, as it now begun to hurt me, and slipped it upon Ayr's finger, asking him to keep it for me till some happier time.

" In the afternoon of the second day, it became evident that the raft was too large for the strength of the
ropes that held it together, and that a smaller one must
be made. Ayr set to work to build it almost alone. Indeed, but four of us were now left — Simpson, an Eng-
lishman, Hobbes the mate, Ayr, and I. Ayr had lost a
great deal of his strength, and his knife slipped from his
hand and sank in the sea. I lent him mine, for the other
two men were destitute of knives; Hobbes had lost his
when Ayr knocked him out of the boat.

" Just as the new raft was ready to be cut loose, a
great sea struck us, and widely separated the two, leaving
Ayr and Hobbes on what remained of the old one, while
Simpson and I were on the new. I saw Ayr plunge
into the water and strike out toward us ; but after a few
strokes he turned back, either because he felt he had not
strength to reach us, or because he would not leave
Hobbes helpless. The sudden night of the tropics shut
down upon us, and when morning dawned the old raft
was nowhere to be seen.

" The sea was now much less violent, and Simpson
and I managed to maintain our position in spite of our
wasted strength. I felt that another night would be our
last. But an hour before sunset we were picked up by a
Dutch vessel, bound on an exploring voyage to the
coasts of Borneo and Celebes. We had not the luck to
sight any vessel going in the opposite direction, and so

could only return after the explorations had been made, which kept us away from home nearly two years longer.

"When at last I crossed my father's threshold again, a week ago, I found that I was not only given up for dead, but was supposed to have been murdered by my dearest friend, Roderick Ayr. He and Hobbes had been picked up by a vessel bound for Liverpool.

"Hobbes, who, it seems, had never given up his grudge against Ayr, passing through my native town on his way from Boston to his own home, had stopped over a train for the purpose of setting afloat the story of the wreck, in which he so far mingled truth and falsehood as to represent that Ayr, in view of the scanty stock of provisions on the raft, had successively murdered three of the men in their sleep,— of whom I was one,— robbed them, and rolled their bodies off into the sea.

"When Ayr came along on the next train, a policeman's hand was laid upon his arm before he stepped off from the platform. He was taken to police headquarters and searched, and as my watch, my ring, and my knife were found in his possession, the evidence against him seemed conclusive. But the living, lying witness had disappeared, and could not be found. Either he had felt that he would be unable to confront Ayr and withstand cross-questioning, or else he had no desire to send Ayr to the gallows, but only to disgrace him in the estimation of his townsmen. In this he succeeded to a considerable extent. Ayr told the straight story, which his nearest friends believed — except some who feared he might have done, under the peculiar temptations of a wreck, what he would not have done under any other circumstances; and as no murder could be actually proved, he, of course, could not be held. But most of the people ominously shook their heads, and refused to receive his account of the watch, the ring, and the knife as anything but an ingenious triple falsehood. It was more than he could stand, and between two days he disappeared, his nearest relatives not knowing what had become of him.

"When I suddenly appeared in the town a few days since, those overwise people of two years ago were dumbfounded, and I hope by this time they are sufficiently ashamed of themselves. But some one besides Roderick Ayr had left the town during my absence. Miss Rogers had removed to Detroit six years before, and I took the next train for that city, only to learn that after a brief residence she had come here. So I retraced my journey.

"As we were entering the city this afternoon, I put my head out of the car-window in an idle way, and thought I saw a strange vision — a man standing beside the track with a flag in his hand, who wore the features of Roderick Ayr. In a moment it was gone, and I could not tell whether it was fancy or reality, whether I had been dreaming or awake. But as I was passing through the door of the railway station he accosted me, and sure enough it was my friend."

" By jolly ! " said Monkey Roe, and brought his fist down upon the table with a whang that made every dish leap up an inch.

" *Johannes in perpetuo !* — Jack for ever ! " said Isaac Holman.

" O-o-o-o-h ! " said Ned, three times — once with his mouth, and once with each eye.

Phaeton leapt to his feet, and waving his napkin over his head, proposed " Three cheers for Roderick Jack-in-the-Box ! " — whereupon all the boys rose instantly and gave three terrific cheers and a handsome tiger.

" Please excuse me, Aunty," said Phaeton ; " I 'm going to bring Jack-in-the-Box," and he was off.

" I don't know what he means by that," said Aunt Mercy. " You see, Edmund Burton, there 's a gentleman connected with the railroad — either president or one of the directors — Monsieur Thibaux, Jacquin Thibaux, originally a Frenchman, who seems to have befriended these boys in some way, and they talk a good deal about him. I always have to laugh at the way they pronounce his name ; as they don't understand French, they call it Jack-in-the-Box. I believe Monsieur Thibaux is a very fine man, but I don't know why my nephew should bring him here."

" The explanation is this," said Miss Glidden, " that Jack-in-the-Box, Jacquin Thibaux, and Roderick Ayr are one and the same person."

" Then of course I shall be most happy to welcome him," said Aunt Mercy. " But I confess I can't understand how a runaway young man could so soon become president of a great railroad, nor why the president should be waving a red flag, like a switch-tender."

The good lady had surpassed both of her nephews in making a muddle, and before it could be cleared up to her satisfaction, Mr. Ayr was announced.

The hostess rose to greet him, and " all the boys except Miss Glidden," as Patsy Rafferty expressed it, made a rush for him and wound themselves around him like an anaconda.

" Where 's Fay ? " said Ned, as he looked about him when the anaconda had loosened its folds.

" He 's at the Box, managing the signals," said Jack.

The hero of the evening was now beset with inquiries, and nearly the whole story was gone over again, by question and answer.

" I understand it all now," said Ned, " except one thing. Why did you always refuse to look at a newspaper ? "

" There were several reasons for that," said Jack. " One was, that the paragraph about my supposed crime was constantly turning up. Another was, that I thought my friends would advertise for me, and was afraid some of them might attempt to decoy me with what they would consider a justifiable fib,— as, that my mother was at the point of death, or something of that sort. If such a thing appeared, I preferred not to see it."

CHAPTER XXII.

OLD SHOES AND ORANGE-BLOSSOMS.

NOT many weeks after the tea party, there were two weddings. Mr. Burton and Aunt Mercy were married on Wednesday quietly at her house, and none of the boys were there except Phaeton and Ned. Roderick Ayr and Miss Glidden were married next morning in church, and all the boys were there.

In the arrangements for this wedding, it was planned that there should be no bridesmaids and no best man, though it was then the fashion to have them,— but four ushers. Jack had asked Phaeton and Ned Rogers, Isaac Holman, and me, to officiate in this capacity ; and we, with a few of the other boys, met in the printing-office to talk it over.

"I suppose we shall get along somehow," said Ned, " but I never ushed in my life, and I would n't like to make any blunder."

"You can buy a behavior-book that tells all about it," said Charlie Garrison.

"I don't much believe in books for such things," said Ned. "I remember once when we were going to take

Uncle Jacob's horse to pasture, Fay sat up half the night reading a book about horseback-riding, and yet when we actually had the horse under us, we did n't get along very well."

"That," said I, "was only because we had n't the proper things. If we had had a Mexican saddle and a gag bit and wheel spurs, we should have galloped over the ground so fast we could hardly have viewed the scenery as we rode by."

"Yes," said Charlie, "and you 'll find you must have a lot of trappings for this affair — white gloves and bouquets, and rosettes and cockades, and bridal favors, and a little club with ribbons on it, to hit the boys when they don't keep still."

"Oh, pshaw!" said Jimmy the Rhymer, "half of those are the same thing. And as for hitting the boys, they 'd better hit the whole congregation, who never know any better than to jump up and gaze around every time there 's a rumor that the bridal party have arrived."

"I don't think we need be troubled about it," said Phaeton. "Of course Jack will rehearse us a little, and instruct us what to do."

"*Bonus ego cervus!* Good idea!" said Holman. "Let 's go up to the Box this afternoon and ask him."

And we agreed that we would.

"That 's all very well for that part of the business," said Jimmy the Rhymer; "but there 's something else

we ought to talk over and agree upon, which we can't ask
Jack about."

"What 's that ? "

" I mean," said Jimmy, " our own demonstration.
Of course we 're not going to stand by and see Jack-in-
the-Box married and disposed of without doing something to show our friendship for him."

" They won't receive any presents," said Holman.

" And I think all the flowers there need be will be
provided by somebody else," said Phaeton.

" Then," said Jimmy, " there is but one thing left
for us."

" What 's that ? "

" Old shoes."

" Old shoes ? "

" Yes.   Don't you know that it 's a famous custom to
throw old shoes after people, as a sign that you wish them
good luck — especially when they 're just married and
starting off on their wedding journey ? "

" I 've heard of it," said Phaeton, " but I never saw it
done."

" I 'll go for that," said Monkey Roe.   " Horseshoes,
or human shoes ? "

" For Roderick Ayr and his beautiful bride, nothing
but the softest velvet moccasins," said the poet.

" Don't believe I can get them," said Monkey.   " We
don't wear that kind at our house."

"I'm afraid it won't do to have any throwing about it," said Holman. "Last week I read a paragraph about a negro wedding where they all threw their old shoes after the couple as they were riding away, and one of them knocked the bridegroom's five-dollar silk hat into the middle of next week, while another broke the bride's jaw."

"Was there a full account of the other ceremonies at that wedding?" said Patsy Rafferty.

"I don't remember," said Holman. "Why?"

"Because," said Patsy, "whatever they did, we must do the very contrary."

"There need n't be any throwing, that 's certain," said Jimmy. "And that will give us a chance to put in an old horseshoe, which is luckier than any other."

"Those carriages," said Phaeton, "generally have a platform behind to carry trunks on. While the bridal party are in the church, we might have all our old shoes piled up on that platform."

"That 's it," said Jimmy. "And that will give us a chance to decorate them with a few flowers and ribbons."

We appointed Jimmy a committee of one to manage the old shoes.

In the afternoon we four who were to be ushers went to see Jack-in-the-Box.

"Jack," said Ned, "if we 're going to ush for you, you 'll have to instruct us a little. None of us under-

stand the science very well, and we 're afraid to try learning it from books."

Jack laughed heartily.

"As to the science of ushing, as you call it," said he,
"it 's a very simple matter."

Then he got a sheet of paper and a pencil, drew
roughly a ground plan of the church, showed us our
places at the heads of the aisles, and gave us all the information that was needed for our simple duties.

"And about the clubs?" said Ned. "Will you
make those? or do we buy them?"

"What clubs?" said Jack.

"The little clubs with ribbons wound around them,"
said Ned, "to hit the boys with when they don't keep
still."

Jack laughed more heartily than before.

"I guess we wont hit the boys," said he. "They
need n't keep any stiller than they want to, at my wedding."

And then he explained to us the difference between a
marshal and an usher.

"A marshal," said he, "is a sort of commander, and
the little club, as you call it, is the symbol of his authority.
But an usher stands in the relation of servant to those
whom he shows to their places.

"I must tell Charlie Garrison about that," said Ned;
"it was he who started the story about the little clubs.

Charlie 's an awful good boy, but he generally gets things wrong. I 'm afraid he 's too ready to believe everything anybody tells him."

In trying to describe Charlie, Ned had so exactly described himself, that we all broke into a smile.

As we were walking away, Holman suggested that perhaps while we were about it we ought to have got instructions as to the reception, also ; for there was to be a brief one at the house immediately after the ceremony in the church.

" Oh, I know all about that," said Phaeton.

" Then let 's hear how it is," said Holman.

" It 's simply this," said Phaeton. " You go up to the couple, and shake hands, and if you 're a girl you kiss the bride — What did you say ? You wish you were ? — and wish them many happy returns of the day ; then you say what kind of weather you think we 've had lately, and the bridegroom says what kind he thinks, and the bride waves her fan a little ; then you give a real good smile and a bow, and go into another room and eat some cake and ice-cream ; and then you go home. That 's a reception."

" It sounds reasonable," said I ; " but I don't feel quite certain about it. I will ask my sisters."

When I asked them, they laughed, but said that if I did as Phaeton had directed, I 'd probably get through safely.

15

Two days before the wedding, Jack resigned his place in the employ of the railroad, and took all his things away from the Box. Patsy Rafferty's father succeeded him as signal-man.

Thursday was a beautiful, dreamy October day, and as we had settled all the weighty questions of etiquette, we put on the white gloves with a feeling of the most dignified importance. The people began coming early. The boys, who were among the earliest, came in a compact crowd, and we gave them first-rate seats in the broad aisle, above the ribbon. Before ten o'clock every seat was filled, and in the steep gallery beauty and fashion were banked up, "like Niobe, all tiers."

Everybody in town seemed to be present. There were matrons with a blush of the spring-time returned to their faces, who must have witnessed scores of weddings and become connoisseurs in all that pertains to them. There were little misses in short dresses, who had never looked on such a spectacle before. There were young ladies evidently in the midst of their first campaign, just a little excited over one of those events toward which ill-natured people say all their campaigning is directed. There were fathers of families, with business-furrowed brows, brushing the cobwebs from dim recollections, and marking the discovery of each with the disappearance of a wrinkle. There were bachelors who, if not like the irreverent hearers of Goldsmith's preacher, were at least likely to go

away with deep remorse or desperate resolve. There
were some who would soon themselves be central figures
in a similar spectacle. There were those, perhaps, whose
visions of such a triumph were destined to be finally as
futile as they were now vivid.

Frequent ripples of good-natured impatience ran
across the sea of heads, and we who felt that we had the
affair in charge began to be a little anxious, till the organ
struck up a compromise between a stirring waltz and a
soothing melody, which speeded the precious unoccupied
moments on their long journey.

The usual number of false alarms caused the usual
automatic turning of heads and eyes. But at last the
bridal party, like the wolf in the fable, really came; and
as they glided up the broad aisle, the bride might almost
have mounted bodily to the seventh heaven on the sub-
stantial stares that were directed at her,— whence perhaps she could have slidden down again on some whispered railing at her want of bridesmaids. But her eyes
were on the ground, and she heard nothing but the rustle
of her own train, and saw nothing, I trust, but the visions
that are dear to every human heart, in spite of the sorrowful comment of human experience.

The organ checked its melodious enthusiasm as the
party reached the chancel. Then the well-known half-
audible words were uttered, with a glimmer of a ring
sliding upon a dainty finger. The benediction was said,

a flourish of the organ sounded the retreat, and the party ran the gauntlet of the broad aisle again, while the audience, as was the fashion of that day, immediately rose to its feet and closed and crushed in behind them, like an avalanche going through a tunnel.

While we were in the church, Jimmy the Rhymer, with Lukey Finnerty to help him, had brought the old shoes in an immense basket, and arranged them on the platform at the back of the bridegroom's carriage. The cluster of seven boots which Patsy had used for a drag to control Phaeton's car, was laid down as a foundation. On this were piled all sorts of old shoes, gaiters, and slippers, bountifully contributed by the boys, and at the top of the pyramid a horseshoe contributed by Jimmy himself. Sticking out of each shoe was a small bouquet, and the whole was bound together and fastened to the platform with narrow white ribbons.

"I wanted to write a little poem for the occasion," said Jimmy to me, the next day, "and tie it to the horseshoe; but somehow when I tried there was a lump in my throat, and the inspiration would n't come."

My young lady readers will want to know what the bride wore. As nearly as I can recollect — and I have refreshed my memory by a glance at the best fashion-magazines — it was a wine-colored serge Sicilienne, looped up with pipings of gros-grain galloon, cut *en train* across the sleeve-section; the overskirt of Pompadour

BRIDAL FAVORS.

passementerie, shirred on with striped gore of garnet silk, the corners caught down to form shells for the heading, and finished off in knife plaitings of brocaded facing that she had in the house. Coiffure a fanchon remnant of pelerine blue, laced throughout and crossing at the belt. The corsage was a pea-green fichu of any material in vogue, overshot with delicate twilled moss-heading cut bias, hanging gracefully in fan outline at the back, trimmed with itself and fitted in the usual manner with darts; bertha panier of suit goods, and Watteau bracelets to match.

With such a costume as this overflowing its open sides, and our contribution on the trunk-board, the carriage presented a very original and picturesque appearance as it rolled away.

The boys went to the reception as they had gone to the tea party and the wedding, in a solid crowd. When we presented ourselves, Ned made us all laugh by literally following his brother's humorous instructions. The caterer thought he had provided bountifully for the occasion; but when the boys left the refreshment-room, he stood aghast. The premium boy in this part of the performance was Monkey Roe.

As Ned and I walked silently toward home, he suddenly spoke:

"It's all right! For the fact is, Miss Glidden was too awful old for Fay and Jimmy and Holman. She's nineteen, if she's a day."

" I 've no doubt of it," said I, " and besides, they could n't all have had her. But how came you to know that about Fay and Jimmy and Holman ? "

I thought Ned had not discovered what I had.

Without a word, he placed his forefinger in the corner of his eye, then pulled the lobe of his ear, and then, spreading the fingers of both hands, brought them carefully together, finger-end upon finger-end, in the form of a cage. By which he meant to say that he could see, and hear, and put this and that together.

" Ah, well ! " said I, " let us not talk about it. We may be nineteen ourselves some day."

THE END.

Scribners' New List

—of—

Books for Young Folks

THE BOY'S KING ARTHUR.

Being Sir THOMAS MALORY'S History of King Arthur and his Knights of the Round Table.

Edited, with an Introduction, by SIDNEY LANIER.

WITH 12 ILLUSTRATIONS BY ALFRED KAPPES.

One Volume 8vo, Extra Cloth - - - - - **$3.00.**

Mr. Sidney Lanier, under the title of THE BOY'S KING ARTHUR, has given the OISSART a companion which perhaps even surpasses it. However familiar the Arian heroes may be to him, as mere names encountered in poetry and scattered legends, t one boy in ten thousand will be prepared for the endless fascination of the great ries in their original shape and vigor of language. He will have something of the ling with which, at their first writing, as Mr. Lanier says in his Preface, the "fascited world read of Sir Lancelot du Lake, of Queen Guenever, of Sir Tristram, of Queen lde, of Merlin, of Sir Gawaine, of the Lady of the Lake, of Sir Galahad, and of the nderful search for the Holy Cup, called the 'Saint Graal.'"

CHARLES SCRIBNER'S SONS, PUBLISHERS,

743 and 745 BROADWAY, NEW YORK.

THE BOY'S FROISSART

Edited, with an Introduction, by SIDNEY LANIER.

WITH ILLUSTRATIONS BY ALFRED KAPPES.

One Volume Crown 8vo, Extra Cloth - - - - - - - $3.00

"As you read of the fair knights and the foul knights, — for Froissart tells of both, it cannot but occur to you that somehow it seems harder to be a good knight nowada than it was then. . . . Nevertheless the same qualities which made a manful fighter the make one now. To speak the very truth; to perform a promise to the utmost; to rev ence all women; to maintain right and honesty; to help the weak; to treat high and l with courtesy; to be constant to one love; to be fair to a bitter foe; to despise luxury; pursue simplicity, modesty, and gentleness in heart and bearing, — this was in the oath the young knight who took the stroke upon him in the fourteenth century, and this still the way to win love and glory in the nineteenth." — EXTRACT FROM THE PREFACE.

***For sale by all booksellers, or will be sent, postpaid, upon receipt of price, by

CHARLES SCRIBNER'S SONS, PUBLISHERS,

743 and 745 BROADWAY, NEW YORK.

A NEW ILLUSTRATED EDITION OF

HANS BRINKER:

Or, THE SILVER SKATES.

A STORY OF LIFE IN HOLLAND.

By Mrs. MARY MAPES DODGE,

Author of " Rhymes and Jingles," and Editor of "St. Nicholas."

WITH TWELVE FULL-PAGE ILLUSTRATIONS.

One Volume, 12mo, Cloth, bevelled edges -   -   -   -   *$1.50.*

HANS BRINKER; or, THE SILVER SKATES, is one of those stories which is
destined to be a source of perennial delight to generation after generation of children. It
tells of life in Holland, a country which changes so little that a story of people who
lived there twenty years ago might be told of to-day as well; and it is marked through
out by a vivacity, a freshness, and a healthy vigor, which goes straight to the heart of
every reader, whether he be old or young.

** *For sale by all booksellers, or will be sent, prepaid, upon receipt of price, by*

CHARLES SCRIBNER'S SONS, PUBLISHERS,

743 and 745 BROADWAY, NEW YORK

JULES VERNE'S LATEST STORY.

The Giant Raft. Part I.

EIGHT-HUNDRED LEAGUES

ON THE AMAZON.

One Vol., Square 12mo, Extra Cloth. - - - - - - - - $1.50

WITH FIFTY FULL PAGE ILLUSTRATIONS.

THE START OF THE JURGADA.

The series of volumes which Jules Verne has brought out with the view of giving an orderly account of the great voyages and explorations of all times is completed with *The Explorers of the Nineteenth Century* In addition to this volume, a new work by the same author is in course of publication. It is entitled *The Giant Raft*, and its scene is laid in South America, the title of the first part being "*Fight Hundred Leagues on the Amazon*." Like the recent "*Steam House*," it is adorned with many spirited illustrations by French artists, and has all the wonderful interest of scenery and incident which Jules Verne knows how to put into all his books.

** For sale by all booksellers, or will be sent, pre-paid, upon receipt of price, by

CHARLES SCRIBNER'S SONS. PUBLISHERS,

743 and 745 BROADWAY, NEW YORK.

www.ingramcontent.com/pod-product-compliance
Lightning Source LLC
Chambersburg PA
CBHW030914270326
41929CB00008B/697